To the love of my life, my wife, Vanessa, who is my biggest cheerleader and the primary reason this book was published. Without her encouragement and oversight, I would have never written it.

THE WAGES OF SINS OF THE SON

Guilty in Mississippi II

PERCY LYNCHARD

Page Solutions
541 Buttermilk Pike
Crescent Springs, KY 41017

ISBN 979-8-89633-123-0 (softcover)
ISBN 979-8-89633-126-1 (hardcover)
ISBN 979-8-89633-125-4 (ebook)

Printed in the United States of America.

CHAPTER 1

Jennifer Garrett played with her pet poodle in the living room of her home in the Roundaway Community of Sunflower County, Mississippi, one of the many rural southern communities much too small to be a town of any type, but with enough people to feel a sense of belonging. Roundaway was in the western corner of the County not far from the Bolivar County line, truly out in the sticks. Jennifer Garrett was 18 years old, a recent graduate of the Class of 1970 at Linn High School and currently attending Mississippi Delta Junior College over in nearby Moorehead, Mississippi. She was nothing short of beautiful and had a body most twenty-two year-olds would give anything to have. To those that knew her, she was sweet as sugar. To those that didn't she was stuck up and a real bitch; the quintessential Southern girl.

"I don't think you have been outside in a while", she said to the dog as if he would answer. "You probably need to go and do your business. We don't need another of your "accidents" in the living room."

Jennifer opened the front door and the dog shot out into the yard as if he had never been out in his life. The darkness swallowed him up, but she wasn't concerned. She had let him out in this manner countless times and there was never a problem. He wouldn't go far and would quickly return she thought. But he didn't. Fifteen or so minutes after she had let him out, she walked into the yard and called for him. Then she called again and yet again. He still didn't return. Concerned but certainly not panicked, she started down the paved road in front of her house to look for him, calling all the while. Before she even realized where she was, she had gone at least a quarter of a mile from her home in the blackness that only rural people know because of the absence of street lights in the country. She was just about to turn around when she saw a white object in the road ten to fifteen yards ahead and ran to it. It was her dog alright, and she dropped to her knees sobbing, already blaming herself for letting the dog get run over apparently, under her watch.

"Pips, I am so sorry," she wailed as she dropped to the ground, picking the dog up and holding it like a newborn child. "I never saw a car pass here," she explained to the dog that lay limp in her arms.

It was then that she noticed that the dog's faux diamond collar was missing from his neck. She had only seconds to ponder that fact when she felt masculine hands encircle her neck and large fingers exert pressure on the front of her throat, followed by immediate terror filling her very soul. She tried to scream but couldn't as the pressure on her throat became more severe. Every time she tried to catch her breath, his fingers sank deeper and deeper into her neck. She felt her eyes bulge and the terror she felt was like the worst nightmare she had ever had geometrically multiplied. She could feel and smell his hot breath on the back of her neck and feel his torso press against her back as he hovered over her as she tried to get up from her crouching position. She tried to pull his hands away from her, but he was much too strong. Her attempts to scratch his arms as he held her were futile as he wore a jacket or thick long sleeve shirt. Ultimately, she felt a strange calmness wash over her and the need to breathe slowly leave her as everything went black and she became one with the darkness.

Though her body was limp and he knew she was dead, the man held on for a while longer to be sure that was the case. When he had convinced himself that her life was over, he let go of her and she dropped into a pile on top of the dead dog. Winded from the assault of the young girl, he sat down next to her and recuperated. After he had done so, he picked her up and carried her several rows deep into the nearby soybean field where he began to strip the body of all her clothes. It was this part that excited him the most and he was barely able to contain himself. In a matter of minutes, the act was over and he dressed himself. He looked over the body for a final time and grabbed the small gold chain with a silver cross attached that she wore around her neck and tore it from her body, thereafter stuffing it into the pocket of his pants. He disappeared into the night as easily as he had appeared, stepping over the dog's body that still lay in the middle of the road.

Jennifer's parents had no idea that she was not in the house until a couple of hours later when her father made a nighttime bathroom run and noticed the light in the living room was still on. When he cut it off, he checked his daughter's bedroom and found she had not gone to bed, so he began to look for her around the house and in the yard. The fact that the dog was also missing, strangely gave him a sense of ease, believing they were together which surely meant they were not far. However, when he found her car still at home, he began to panic and immediately called the sheriff's office in nearby Indianola, the county seat of Sunflower County. He awakened his wife and Jennifer's mother, Wilma, and told her of the girl's absence which initially angered Wilma for her daughter leaving the house without permission in the middle of the night, but then she felt guilt and great concern for the girl's safety after she was awake for a few minutes.

She got up from bed and assisted her husband with the cursory search of the home and yard and was sill outside when the sheriff's department arrived at their home after Sammy had called them. Wilma went back into the house as the deputy had instructed her shortly thereafter, leaving Sammy to deal with the authorities and get the official search started. The truth be known, she was much too emotional about the possibility of something happening to her daughter to be of much real assistance anyway. She couldn't imagine where her angel had gone without her car and could only consider that foul play was involved because Jen would never do something like run away or go anywhere without letting them know. She had to be at work early the next morning at the post office in nearby Doddsville, but couldn't think of sleep at the moment without knowing where her daughter was.

Nothing attracts the attention of the people of a small community like the flashing lights of an emergency vehicle, be it law enforcement, fire truck or ambulance. First of all, in the Mississippi Delta they can be seen for several miles across the flat fields and virtually treeless landscape. Secondly, since everyone in those numerous rural communities knew everyone, there was genuine concern for the safety and welfare of their neighbors. Within a matter of a single hour, everyone within a five-mile radius of Roundaway knew that Jennifer Garrett was missing and that her dog had apparently been run over. Within another thirty minutes, everyone knew she was dead, murdered at the hands of a predator. Her rape was held in confidence by the Sheriff's deputies and investigators as a courtesy to her family for the time being, but also to hold some cards close to their chest pending further investigation. Her body was removed by ambulance and taken to the morgue at the East Bolivar County Hospital in nearby Cleveland, Mississippi, the only morgue available to Sunflower County residents at the time.

Detective Taylor Buttrell was in charge of the investigation and worked the scene of the murder on that night. He had met another deputy at the Garrett home not long after the call had come into the sheriff's office that the girl was missing. When he began a perimeter search of the area around the home, much as her father had done, he expanded it and very quickly found the dead family pet in the road a short distance from the house. When he searched the area around the dog's body, he found drag marks leading into the soybeans and almost immediately found the girl's body.

"Dammit," he said out loud to no one. A search for a teenage runaway had instantly turned into a murder investigation and he was none too pleased with the thought of informing her parents that she was dead, a task he had performed on multiple occasions during his career, but one that never got easier despite the repetitions.

"Horace, get a fifty-yard perimeter around the body roped off and allow no one inside until the DA's office gets here," Taylor ordered one of the deputies. "And have enough pictures made of this scene so that the stock in Kodak rises to a record high," he barked.

"Be better for the pictures if we waited 'til morning when there was more light", the deputy responded.

"We can take more then, but we ain't about to leave this body here 'til morning," Taylor said. Unless you're volunteering to go tell her parents she's dead out here and we'll get her moved in the morning". The deputy hung his head and started getting the camera ready.

"I didn't think so," Taylor said. "As bad as I hate to, I'm heading to the house to do it."

Taylor approached the home and found both parents in the front yard. He asked them to come into the house and sat down with them at the breakfast table inside. "I'm sorry to be the bearer of bad news, Mr. and Mrs. Garrett, but it seems that your daughter was attacked a short distance from the house and was killed. I have already called for a transport from the coroner for her to be taken to Cleveland until some funeral home arrangements can be made. "I want to see her now", demanded Sammy. "I'm afraid you can't, Mr. Garrett" Taylor told him. I have the area where she was found roped off and can't let anyone near it because of the need to preserve evidence." Wilma wailed and Sammy broke down himself at that point. "Find the son of a bitch, Mr. Buttrell and let me have him before you take him in", Sammy told him. Both he and his wife got up and walked outside into the night, looking down the road toward the activity by emergency personnel. "Who would want to hurt our darling daughter", questioned Wilma. "How will I live without her"? Taylor did his best to console the two to no avail and even contacted a victim assistant from the DA's office to come out to sit with them for a while. When she arrived, Taylor excused himself and headed to the morgue after first having one or both of the parents to come to the East Bolivar County Hospital morgue in Cleveland to identify the body. When Sammy agreed, Taylor left, not looking forward to their meeting again in Cleveland later.

CHAPTER 2

Paul Lane was reared back in his chair in his office opposite the street from the Bolivar County Courthouse in Cleveland, Mississippi, trying to concentrate, on work, but instead caught himself admiring the huge statue of the confederate soldier that stood on the front lawn of the courthouse instead. Six or seven years out of law school, he couldn't remember which without looking at his diploma, he was comfortable in his life. As an investigator for the District Attorney of the 11th Circuit Court District of Mississippi in 1970, he was making upwards of twenty thousand dollars per year with insurance and retirement benefits from the state, much more than the average young lawyer in the Delta unless they hit the jackpot on some personal injury cases and garnered a hefty fee. A person's misfortune was a lawyer's gain in the legal world. He had been employed with the DA for several years and thoroughly enjoyed his job, unlike practicing law in his early years. He had grown up here and little could be said that wasn't positive about his life. Good money, a new house in the country and an attractive girlfriend. Sure, there were a few things about his success as an investigator that stuck in his craw, a few cases he had yet to conclude that perhaps he should have, but for the most part, very few would consider him anything but successful. In a rural town like Cleveland or

Bolivar County, Mississippi, he knew most everybody and everybody knew him.

Paul was born in the Delta, educated in the Delta at Cleveland High School and Delta State College, and had secured his roots deeply there with his employment and recent purchase of a home. Had there been a law school at Delta State, he would have probably have gone there but since there was not, he had attended and graduated from Ole Miss Law School in nearby Oxford. He was a true blue Deltan and that helped his career tremendously as Delta people are often distrustful of or prone to dislike outsiders, and an outsider to most people in that region would be anyone who had never lived in the Delta at any time in their lives for a period of at least five years or more. To some an outsider was anyone who wasn't born in the Delta. It is often said that there is one thing that terrified citizens of Mississippi and especially those in the Delta more than anything else in the world, and that was a Yankee with a U-Haul headed south down Highway 61. Outsiders were not generally welcome at all in Mississippi and in the Delta perhaps less than normal. Forget that Mississippi was called "The Hospitality State" in its tourism brochures. Either way, Paul fit the mold of a Mississippi Deltan perfectly by not only having the pedigree, but also the other credentials.

Paul was basically waiting on lunch time to come as he sat at his desk. It was too close to the noon hour to start anything related to work and he had finished writing reports on some dope cases that he had investigated and were nearing the time for preliminary hearings or presentation to the upcoming grand jury. He could go ahead and go to lunch if he wanted, but he was particularly interested in making his secretary wait until noon and not leave early herself. She had done that in the past and he needed to put a stop to it before it became her routine. Gotta give the taxpayers a full day of work for a full day's pay, he surmised. She wouldn't dare leave early with him there and he knew it.

Stalling for time actually let him continue to work on reports and go through phone messages. He thumbed through them and found one that piqued his interest more than the others, which appeared to be the typical calls from law enforcement officers asking about the upcoming grand jury session and those from property crime victims who were asking about the status of their case and the possible return of their property. This one was different. It was from the sheriff's office over in neighboring Sunflower County. A detective by the name of Taylor Buttrell wanted to talk to him about the "Interstate murders", the murders of two girls in Bolivar County that was unsolved. Paul had talked to Taylor in the past on some other cases, but had not done so in several months. His heart sank as he recalled the murders of Linda Strawberry and Janice Galtelli last year, both by strangling in the rural community of Interstate in southeast Bolivar County, very near the Sunflower County line. His failure to solve those murders was a sore subject to him, but he had mixed emotions about it if that was what Taylor was calling about. First and foremost, it could mean that an animal masquerading as a human had come out of hiding and was stalking more victims. That would be disheartening. However, it may also mean that the killer might have gotten sloppy and left some clues that they could go on because he sure hadn't done so in the first two murders. He continued to flip through the phone messages and found yet another call from Taylor Buttrell. This one simply read: "Can you meet with me and bring your Interstate Murders file?" It was in fact the murders he had been unable to solve and Paul felt queasy. His mind reeled with the images of each slain girl, both beautiful and young, murdered in their own homes and laying across both of their beds, nude, strangled to death and raped post mortem. No fingerprints anywhere, no forced entry in either case and the apparent murder weapon being a nylon stocking in the first case belonging to the Strawberry victim and the Galtelli victim's own belt used to strangle her in the second, both within only a few days of each other. No established motive in either case except pure animal lust and a need for violence. Nothing taken or disturbed in either home except possibly one ring belonging to each victim that the perpetrator had probably taken as a souvenir. One was a small diamond cluster ring taken from the Galtelli victim and the other a ring with a triple opal setting taken from the Strawberry victim. Definitely the work of the same predator, but other than that, nothing else to go on. As was the custom in crimes involving the theft of personal property, he had sent out descriptions of the ring from each case to the local pawn shops as stolen, in the hope that the thief or in this case the murderous thief might try to unload them. The odds were against it., but it was the only possible or foreseeable lead they might get. For obvious reasons the fact that the rings were taken from a murder crime scene was withheld from the public. As he recalled the image of the murdered and raped body of each girl sprawled out nude and dead on their own beds, Paul wasn't sure if he was hungry anymore. Putting off the famous Keene Freeze slaw burgers for another few minutes, he called the detective in Sunflower County.

"Taylor this is Paul Lane over in Cleveland returning your call. How's it going?"

"Same shit, different day," Taylor chirped back. "Got a case you might be interested in over here that has all the markings of your Interstate community murder case from a year or so ago. Got time to compare case files?"

"Always my man, always. Whatcha got about two this afternoon? I can meet you there or you can come here," Paul answered.

"Let me come there. I need to get away from the office and clear my mind a little," Taylor responded. "My case anyway at this point."

"Meet you here at two then. My conference room," Paul returned, then hung up the phone and headed out the door to the Keene Freeze.

Again, the mixed emotions caused him anxiety as he recalled the frustrations from the earlier murder investigations along with the thought that the murderer may have again reared his head in his county or at least nearby, coupled with the hope that this could be a break for him in the case as well. Either way, there was no use speculating. Two p.m. and the planned meeting would come soon enough. Even the finest hamburgers in Bolivar County with the delicious mustard based slaw for which they were famous couldn't ease his mind or the anxiety he felt. He had served a short stint as a public defender and represented an assortment of scumbags, on both misdemeanors and felonies and enjoyed the challenge of representing them though he knew they were more often than not, guilty as charged. However, homicides were different. How one person could coldly take another's life was without a doubt the very edge of insanity, but certainly not in the legal sense of the word. Serial killers as they would soon begin to be called, by law enforcement as well as the media were in a class of their own. Methodical killers who killed for the sake of killing on multiple occasions were unheard of in the state of Mississippi in the past, but it certainly appeared that was exactly what was stalking the Mississippi Delta in 1969 with the Interstate murders and definitely so now in 1970 if what Taylor had in Sunflower County was similar. His mouth was dry and the pit of his stomach was nauseated at the thought. He knew that he and his law enforcement brothers in Bolivar County were about to be accused of contributing to the victim's death now due to their failure to identify and apprehend the killer last year. He said a silent prayer asking God to at least let this murderer now be somebody else and not the same perpetrator from August of 1969. Then he felt guilty for praying that another murderer was out and about instead of praying that the case that Sunflower County had was not. Murder at all, but perhaps an accident or some other reasonable explainable death. He quickly grew tire of his own speculation and wondering and simply wished that his meeting with detective Taylor Buttrell would come quickly.

CHAPTER 3

At 2:00 P.M., right on time as agreed, a Sunflower County Sheriff's car pulled up in front of Paul's office across from the Bolivar County courthouse and Detective Taylor Buttrell got out and proceeded to the front door, his sunglasses fogging over after sitting in the air conditioned car during the drive over from Indianola and then getting out into the Delta heat and humidity. He was let in by Linda, Paul's secretary and ushered to the conference room where Paul met him. After both men scattered their files across the conference table, both took a chair with Paul going over the details of the Galtelli and Strawberry Interstate Woods murders from a year ago.

"Two young women, ages 17 and 23 were found dead in their bedrooms within mere days of each other. Neither crime scene had any evidence of forced entry into their home. No physical evidence whatsoever, such as, fingerprints, footprints and the like were found at either scene. They had lived within three miles of each other, not five miles from the home of Jennifer Garrett and there was no evidence either of the two girls in Interstate knew each other or had any common friend or social acquaintances. Both had been strangled by some type of ligature, a belt and a nylon stocking and both raped post mortem. It appears a souvenir was taken by the perpetrator in each case, though.

A diamond cluster ring from one victim and another ring with a triple opal setting from the other. That's about it", Paul concluded. That was all Paul had, unfortunately

Detective Butrell countered, "More similarities to my case than I was hoping to find. Tell me what you think, Paul." First of all, all three victims lived within a five mile radius of the other. All three were strangled to death, but my girl shows no evidence of a ligature being used according to the initial autopsy report I received over the phone from the pathologist in Jackson. Interestingly however, she had been raped post mortem. She was 18 years old and had an article of jewelry, a gold chain and a silver or white gold cross missing from around her neck., according to her parents" Buttrell added. "A number of dissimilarities existed, however. She was attacked outside of her home at night on a remote road she lived on while apparently playing with her dog or maybe letting him out to go to relieve himself." We initially thought the dog had been run over because it was killed as well, but there appears to be no broken bones. He apparently strangled the dog as well according to Dr. Wiggins, DVM, here in Cleveland." He said. I think we have one bad hombre out there, whether it's the same person or a copycat killer" Paul chimed in. Too many similarities to discount not being the same perpetrator, could be a copycat killer if he knew the specifics of the Galtelli and Strawberry murders. The manner of death, the age of the victim as well as the post mortem rape was well known by media and individuals close to the family, but the taking of jewelry from each victim as an apparent souvenir is not known to anybody except within the inner circle of the investigation and prosecution team.

CHAPTER 4

Anyone who ever taught school knew Randy Butler or at least someone just like him. He sat in the back of the class and the only time you ever heard from him was when he acted out by cutting up with other students who fit the similar mold as him. Though you could never convince him otherwise, he was far from stupid. Quite the contrary he was very intelligent and could make great grades in any subject if he would just apply himself, but he seldom did without extra encouragement. He never got that at home and if he got it at all, it came from the teacher. He thought of himself as a loser because that's what he was told at home, time and again, from a mother who resented him because his birth had all but put an end to her party scenes and from a father who found his joy floating in the bottom of a glass, his primary escape from long hours of shift work at his job. As far as Randy was concerned, if he looked up the word "loser" in the dictionary, his picture would be there as an illustration. You couldn't help but feel sorry for him although he did seem to fray your last nerve at times as a teacher, thought Mrs. Ferretti, his home room and 8th grade Geography teacher. He had told her once when she tried to get him interested in the study of Latin American geography, that he didn't need to know this stuff because his daddy had often told him the only thing his future held with reference to geography was a trip to Vietnam after he was drafted in a few years. Maybe that was indeed true, she had thought, since here in 1970, that did seem to be where a lot of boys were headed, but she couldn't believe a father would be that cruel to his son. She recalled an incident she had heard once a year or so ago about Randy's father, once in a drunken stupor, had decided Randy needed a haircut and had all but cut him bald with an electric shaver, but leaving uneven strips of hair across his head. Randy had come to school one day wearing a ball cap and she had ordered him to remove it while in class. When he did so and she saw the reason for wearing it, she allowed him to put it back on and later was told the story of his miserable haircut.

Randy was at it again this morning, making jungle animal sounds in the back of the class which drew laughter from the other students as she talked about the Brazilian Rainforest to her class. She scolded him, but held back from sending him to the principal for his weekly paddling because she knew the attention he was now getting was all the attention he would likely receive from anybody. Besides, school would be out in about thirty minutes, anyway. When that long anticipated dismissal bell rang, the students ran out the door, eager to get home. Randy led the pack on his way to the bus for the short ride from Shaw to Interstate Woods, where he lived. His buddy, Wesley, who carried the nickname "Weasel" was right there with him. They were inseparable, which was not always good, at least for the teachers as both seemed to get into mischief and it was hard to tell who was the instigator. On the way, Randy shyly spoke to Olivia a fellow classmate and the girl of his dreams, though she was totally unaware of that fact. On the bus ride home, being harvest season in the Delta, he and Wesley counted cotton pickers and combines in the fields between Shaw and Interstate, a distance of about seven miles. When Randy got home, he ran inside the house and threw his books onto the couch and went to the fridge for a snack, where he met his Dad in a tank top style T-shirt and boxers. Only then did he remember that his Dad was working the graveyard shift this week and had been trying to catch some sleep until Randy had burst onto the scene from the bus. He was not a happy camper and berated his son for the noise that had woke him. He ordered Randy out of the house and told him not to come back in until he was called.

Out in the Delta heat at 4:00 pm, Randy got his bike out and promptly rode to Wesley's house, about a mile away. When the two linked up, they rode together on their bikes toward the only place that housed a coca cola machine in the area, that being the Interstate Baptist Church, about two miles further to the east of them. Both attended there, albeit sporadically, but they knew the church was always open and the machine was accessible to them. They each had some change, so they were good. When they arrived they were hot, tired and thirsty. They went inside to the machine only to find that the price for a drink had been raised to fifty cents and the two had forty five cents between them.

"What now?" asked Randy. "I guess we go without," replied Wesley. "Bull hockey!" was Randy's reply to that. "Let's look around." They searched the pews in the sanctuary and then the Sunday school classrooms, but found nothing laying around.

The pastor's study was just down the hall and Randy surmised that the Pastor may have some loose change they could "borrow", so they went in, finding the door unlocked. Randy opened the middle drawer of the Pastor's desk and ran his hand inside. Nothing to be found. Nothing except a plastic zip lock bag that Randy withdrew. No change there, but it did contain two rings, one, a small diamond cluster, the other with a triple opal setting. The boys had no idea what an opal was, but seeing the diamond cluster, they thought it must be worth hundreds of dollars at the pawn shop in Cleveland, maybe thousands, even. Though neither boy had ever stolen anything in their lives, this was more temptation than either could resist. Randy stuffed the bag with the rings in his jeans and both he and Wesley hightailed it to their bikes and were gone in the twinkling of an eye. On the way home, they agreed that they would never speak of this to anyone. Wesley wanted none of the ill-gotten gains, but Randy set a course on getting to the pawn shop in Cleveland and selling the rings for whatever he could get. He didn't need the money for anything in particular, but this seemed to be a gifted opportunity that might never present itself again and he needed to take advantage of it. When he arrived back at his home, he quietly went back inside despite his father's earlier warning and began to work on his homework from school. As he picked up his books to place them on the kitchen table, he clumsily dropped one to the floor which jarred his father from his sleep and he came into the room like a wild animal. Before Randy could apologize or explain, his father slapped him across his face, sending him sprawling into the kitchen floor. He scrambled to his feet crying and dodged a kick that his father threw at him just in time.

"Where the hell you been?" "And why are you back inside? I told you to stay outside until I called for you," his father said. Raymond Butler was a classic redneck and a bully to his son and children. He was separated from his wife currently and had been for about six weeks. He was desperately trying to make the dating scene as he could see no reason why he wouldn't be desirable to any woman. After all, he was not quite fifty, slightly overweight, balding and had a good paying job. Who wouldn't want him with those statistics. He was a fine catch, or so it seemed to him to him at least. Forget the fact that he drove a 1963 dodge Valiant and a Ford pickup with four wheel drive and had three children ranging in ages from eight to fifteen and a small clap board sided Jim Walter Home in need of numerous repairs, including a new roof, not to mention a drinking problem, he had to be every white trash woman's dream come true.

Ruby, his wife, had left him and the kids several weeks back after they fought when he came home drunk again. She had filed for divorce on the grounds he was a drunk and cruel to her. Though he had been served with divorce papers a week or so ago, he had yet to talk to a lawyer about responding to it, but he still had time.

Randy picked himself up and fled into the yard crying. He had gotten to the point where he really despised his dad, and why not? He blamed him for his mother being gone from his life which was mostly true, but she probably would have left regardless in the future. Truth be known, she missed the single life without the responsibilities of children. Raymond had just hastened her decision to leave.

Randy sat alone under a pecan tree in the side yard of the home, cursing his father silently under his breath. He got a drink of water from a garden hose that lay coiled up next to the house where the faucet was located. He didn't dare go back inside until he was certain his Dad was back asleep. He stretched out under the tree and was soon asleep himself, his ears still ringing from the earlier slap from his dad. Randy was awakened by the sound of a vehicle's tires crunching the gravel drive at their home. He immediately recognized the car as belonging to his mother and she was driving. He ran to talk to her before she got out.

"Is Raymond at work?" she asked.

"No, he's asleep," Randy replied.

"I thought he was working second shift this week," she countered, "leaving at 4:00 or 4:30".

"Not this week, Randy added, Working midnights".

I'm leaving then," Ruby said. "Just wanted to get some shoes I left, but I don't need them that bad."

When are you going to Cleveland? Randy asked her. I need a ride to the pawn shop to see if I can sell some rings I found".

I'll get you one day next week and take you to Cleveland," she told her son as she started to back out of the driveway.

With that she was gone as quickly as she had arrived. Randy lay back against the tree and thought of all the money he might get for the rings he had "found".

The next morning on the bus on the way to school, Randy and Weasel talked for the first time since their previous day's rendezvous at the church. Forgetting for the moment their previous day's agreement to never talk about the incident again, Randy told him of his plans for next week to go to the pawn shop in Cleveland to sell their recently acquired bounty.

"You sure you don't want any of the money?" Randy asked.

"Hell no. That stuff will be poison, I promise," Weasel replied. "God will get you for stealing from the church."

With that, the subject was changed, but Randy thought hard about what Weasel had said for a long time afterwards. This could be more money than Randy had ever had in his life and though he knew the way he got it was not right, he wanted it. He was tired of being looked down upon as a poor kid. People who commit crimes such as theft or burglary always have reasons they believe they were justified in in so doing and Randy was no different, even though he knew better. Social status in the Mississippi Delta, even for a fifteen year old kid meant everything. Randy understood that better now than ever because of the current state of school desegregation in the Mississippi Delta. Just the prior year, U.S. District Judge William Keady for the Northern District of Mississippi had ruled on a number of cases that virtually wiped out desegregation in Delta schools, greatly redrawing school districts and combining black schools with white schools and forever putting to rest the theory that freedom of choice was acceptable when it came to what school a student would attend. What this did virtually overnight was caused numerous private schools or academies to spring up across the Delta which meant any white student whose family could afford it would to go to a private school and would mercifully not have to go to school with the niggers, leaving the public schools to the blacks and poor whites for the most part, thus further defining and widening the social class for families in the Delta. While many of Randy and

Weasel's friends left for Bayou Academy in nearby Skene, Mississippi just west of Cleveland, he and his two siblings, a sister and brother, remained in the very integrated Shaw High School they had always attended which also contained grades 1 through 9.

CHAPTER 5

Ruby Butler pulled into the drive of her former marital home on Trunkline Road in Interstate Woods and sounded the car's horn bringing a very agitated Raymond Butler to the front porch.

"Hey, Bitch, I'm not a field nigger you can get to the car by blowing the horn. What the hell you want, anyway"? he asked. "I want Randy to go with me for an hour or so," she yelled out the window of the car as she then started to get out.

Ruby was dressed up, or at least as dressed up as she ever was. She was the definitive redneck woman for which Mississippi was famous. In her mid-thirties, she wore her dresses way too short and her tops cut way too low. She generally wore enough makeup for two teenagers and always had her nails painted and polished to a high red sheen. The amount of costume jewelry she wore would set off any metal detector she tried to pass through and spoke with a raspy voice caused by many years of smoking, a habit she had picked up as a teenager.

"Good. About time your sorry ass took some time with the kids," he said.

"Did you get the divorce papers yet?" she inquired.

"Damn sure did. You'll hear from my lawyer soon enough," he replied. "Don't guess you want to try to settle it do you?" she asked further. "Naw let the lawyers do it" he responded. "I'd rather give the money to a lawyer than for you to get it", he stated in typical redneck fashion and logic, a typical Mississippi divorce except there was no heavily mortgaged mobile home involved, but either way a classic **_Bubba vs. Bubbette_** case.

Randy came out of the house and got in the front seat of the car next to his mother. She told Raymond she'd be back with him in about an hour or two at the most and backed out of the drive and headed west toward Highway 61 and Cleveland.

"Let's go to Perry's Pawn Shop just inside the city limits on 61" he stated.

In a matter of fifteen minutes they pulled into the gravel parking lot of Perry's used cars and pawn shop.

Randy burst from the car and ran into the business. Mr. Perry, the smooth talking likeable owner, sat on a stool behind a counter with a number of guns in a rack behind him, drinking an RC Cola. The glass counter in front of him had numerous pieces of jewelry, including rings in it on display for sale.

"Whatcha need kid?" Perry asked Randy. I got some rings I need to sell", Randy replied, pulling the plastic bag containing the rings from his pocket and handing it to the Perry.

"Not hot, are they?" Perry inquired. For a brief second Randy nearly backed out of the scheme which in retrospect would have been a great thing, but he didn't. "Oh, no sir, I got them from my Dad's night stand drawer. He and Mom are getting a divorce and he wants to get rid of them, he partially lied."

Perry looked closely at them with a jeweler's glass as well as his naked eye. After a few minutes he said "$20 for the opal and $25 for the diamond, no more". Randy was obviously disappointed and countered "I need at least a hundred for the diamond and fifty for the opal."

"Forty five for both and not a penny more," Perry responded. "Give it to me," Randy said, knowing he was beat but with no point to argue. Perry went to the cash box and took out two twenties and a five and handed it to Randy along with a form for him to fill out and sign which he completed and signed on the counter with a pen that Perry also gave him. The form had Randy's name and address and a statement he signed under oath that he was the owner of the rings involved and they were not stolen. With paperwork completed, he stuffed the cash in his pocket and ran out to his mom's waiting car.

"How much did you get?" Ruby asked her son. "Forty five dollars for two rings", he replied. "Good Lord", she said. "Where did you get them?" she finally asked of him.

"I found them in Dad's nightstand", he said, basically the same lie he had told Perry.

"Does your Daddy know you got them?" she inquired. "I guess he does, but he didn't care" was the answer "Were they his old rings?" she asked further. Randy said "no" and then went on to describe them to his mother. When she appeared to grow angry and started to ask him who he bought the rings for and if he was dating someone, Randy became very nervous. "He's obviously spending a lot of money on some woman, but you don't know who it is, huh?" she stated and asked. "No ma'am, we really haven't talked about it." That was closest to the truth as anything he had said.

The two rode along in silence all the way back to the house. Randy was glad when she let the subject go, however. Back in Cleveland, David Perry was on the phone to the Sheriff's office. "This is David Perry. Can I speak to a deputy about some possibly stolen items I just took in at the pawn shop?" He inquired. Something about the ring purchase didn't seem just right. He was transferred to the DA's office to speak with Paul Lane. When he spoke to Paul about the rings and described them, the phone went deathly silent on the other end. Paul's heart was in his throat. He had waited for this news for over a year now. Trying not to get excited too quickly he made sure the pawn broker had gotten the personal info from the seller about how to contact him. When he described Randy Butler, Paul's heart sank. A typical fifteen year old kid was probably not likely to be his suspect, simply because of his physical characteristics but at least it was a start. He instructed David Perry not to talk with anyone about the rings and of course, to hang onto them as they would be evidence in a criminal investigation. When Paul hung up the phone, he called the sheriff's office to line up a deputy to go with him to the pawn shop and then out to Interstate to see Randy Butler. In a matter of minutes, he and Chief Deputy Joel were in his car heading to Perry's place of business and then south down Highway 61 toward Interstate Woods. While out at Perry's they took the rings from him and gave him a receipt to hold them until needed at trial

CHAPTER 6

Thinking through what they were about to do, they considered the fact that he was a juvenile and subject to certain safeguards and rights accordingly. He probably wasn't the murderer, but he certainly could be involved in the murders as an accessory before or after the fact and they would hate to lose the opportunity to prosecute him, even under Youth Court laws due to their procedural errors in questioning him. Deciding it best to have his parent or parents present, they decided to find his mother and continued on down to the address given on the pawn shop form to find her and then talk to Randy with her present as required with juveniles. They apparently disturbed Raymond Butler's day off when they got to the house and he was none too happy. When asked where Randy was, he told them he didn't know, but told them he had left earlier with his Mother. When asked where she might be found, he told them to check Oliver's Lounge in Shaw.

"She spends most of her time there since we separated," he volunteered, never thinking to ask why the law might want to talk to his son.

The two headed down to Shaw and found Ruby at Oliver's Bar and Grill on Highway 61 just as Raymond had predicted. She sat at the bar nursing a gin and tonic. When asked about her son's whereabouts, she told them she had dropped him off at his father's house a couple hours ago. Now the two investigators glanced at each other as if they smelled a rat emanating from the father who surely lied to them earlier as to Randy's whereabouts.

When she inquired about their reason for wanting to talk to him, both men sidestepped the question and said it was routine on a matter they were looking into. That seemed to satisfy her and she agreed to bring him to Paul's office the next day, at 10:00 in the morning to answer some questions. "I hope he's not in trouble, he's really a good kid, you know," she stated in typical maternal fashion. Both men excused themselves, promising to not be too long in the morning at their planned meeting with her and her child.

As they rode back north on Highway 61 toward Cleveland, the two law enforcement men talked about the planned meeting with young Randy Butler in the morning and what their objectives were. Paul was adamant that they had to know where this kid happened to come by two rings from victims in the most notorious murders to come out of Bolivar in history. Then the light bulb came on in both their heads. Perhaps they were getting the cart before the horse. They needed to get confirmation from family members that these were in fact the victims' rings. They had personally examined them earlier at Perry's and they certainly fit the description of those taken from the murder victims, but they needed confirmation from someone who could be certain. Janice Galtelli's family lived in Jackson, too far to get confirmation before tomorrow morning, but Linda Strawberry's family lived right there in Bolivar County, not far from their current location near Shaw. Turning onto Trunkline Road, they were at the Strawberry residence in a matter of minutes. Linda's mother, Estelle, was not there but was at a local beauty shop having her hair done according to Carolyn, her surviving daughter. She was able to be reached by phone, so Paul called her with the news. Overjoyed to hear they may have a lead after all this time, she happily agreed to come by Paul's office early in the morning and take a look at the opal ring to see if she could positively identify it as the one her daughter wore up until her death. If one ring was identified as belonging to a victim, odds were that the other one belonged to the other victim as well. They could get a positive ID another time for the diamond cluster.

When they got back to Cleveland, Paul's secretary, Linda, had a message from Ruby Butler for him. He called her back at the number she left for him, having to go through the operator because it was a long distance call to Shaw from Cleveland. When she answered, she blurted out to him, "Mr. Lane if this is about those rings Randy sold today, you might want to talk to my husband Raymond as well, because that's where Randy said he got them." Paul could only say, "Thank you. Ma'am, we will talk in the morning", neither confirming or denying that the rings were the subject of their inquiry.

After the end of the phone call, he and Detective Joel high fived each other and immediately started some research on Raymond Butler as well as expressing hope that the opal ring would be positively identified as previously belonging to Linda Strawberry in the morning. It was Miller time and the two headed to a local watering hole, not to celebrate just yet, but to unwind. Why cold beers tasted better at the end of a workday was anybody'd guess, but was certainly the case here. The Thicket was jumping at the end of the day and start of the weekend with apparently every tractor, combine and cotton picker driver in the county in attendance. Paul ordered a hamburger teak with onions and gravy with a side of large steak fries while Joel opted for a hamburger. It was stacked high with lettuce, tomato and an onion slice with cheddar cheese holding it all together. Not the quality that the Keene Freeze sold, but. Damn good burger anyway for a traditionalist like Chief Joel.

CHAPTER 7

Though it was early September, the weather in Mississippi was like early August, but at least there were hopes of cooler times ahead very shortly. School had started, so fall had to be near. Chief Deputy Joel and Paul Lane sat around Paul's conference table the next morning where Paul and Taylor Buttrell had sat just a few days before discussing the very case they were investigating this morning. They had just gotten a call from Mrs. Strawberry who would later confirm with mixed emotions that the opal ring that was sold to Perry's Pawn Shop was indeed the ring her murdered daughter wore up until her death and had been presumptively taken by her assailant. When Paul refused to disclose any further details concerning the reappearance of the ring after a year, she quit inquiring, but she did agree not to discuss its appearance with anyone. When Paul's office doorbell rang, presumptively announcing the arrival of Ruby Butler and her son, Randy, the man of the hour. As Paul answered the door, he was pleased to see that was indeed the case. He immediately sized up young Randy who was about 5 foot 4 inches tall and weighed approximately 150 pounds. As Paul had imagined, likely, much too small to manhandle the young female victims as they had been. His mother walked in behind him, dressed in short shorts and a tight fitting tube top that showed off her bosom, hoop earrings rattling as she walked. They were shown to the conference room and introductions to all present were made. A reel to reel tape recorder sat in the center of the table. Paul hit the power button and the reels began to slowly turn. He began to dictate. "Today is Saturday Sepember,19 and the time is 10:25 a.m. Present is Paul Lane, investigator for the District attorney's office for the 11th Circuit District of Mississippi, Chief Deputy James Joel of the Bolivar County Sheriff's office, Randy Butler, age 15 of Interstate Woods in Bolivar County and his mother, Ruby Butler of Shaw, Mississippi. Have I stated everything correctly, Mrs. Butler? "I believe you have", she answered.

"Do I have your permission to ask your son, Randy, some questions, ma'am?" Paul inquired further. "Yes, you may", she chimed. With that, Paul proceeded. The record will reflect that the minor and his mother have both been sworn to tell the truth.

Paul: "State your name for me, son."

Randy: "Randy Butler"

Paul: "Where and with whom do you live at this time?"

Randy: Trunkline Road, Interstate. I live with my father, Raymond Butler."

Ruby Butler: "That is by agreement. Me and Raymond are separated, but he doesn't have custody of him," Ruby was quick to point out, the stigma of a mother not having custody of her child in this day and time pouring forth.

Paul: "That is fine. How long have you lived with just your father?"

Randy: "About a month, since early August of this year, I think".

Paul: "Who else lives there with you?"

Randy: "Just my younger brother and sister", but they sometimes stay with my grandmother as well.

Paul: "Has anyone else lived there since your mother has been gone?"

Randy: "No sir, but my dad has had some friends over to spend the night at times."

Paul: "Who would that be?"

Randy: "Jizelle, a time or two."

Paul: "Who is that?" "Do you know a last name for her?"

Randy: "No, sir, I guess his girlfriend, I don't know."

Paul: "Does she leave clothes or personal items at the house that you know of, Randy?"

Randy: "None except earrings I can remember."

Paul: "No rings?"

Randy: "None I've ever seen."

Paul: "Randy, you recently sold a couple of rings at Perry's Used cars and Pawn shop. Do you remember that a few days ago?"

Randy: "Oh yes sir." Randy's heart now rested in the middle of his throat, He was ready to throw up at any minute, particularly after the next question.

Paul: "Tell me where you got those rings."

Randy: "Like I told Mr. Perry, I got them from my Dad's nightstand drawer. I found them while I was looking for change to get a coke and thought he must have bought them for Jizelle as a gift or maybe to get married and I didn't want him to give them to her. I want him and my mom to get back together, he partially lied."

Paul: "When was this?"

Randy: "Probably 3 weeks ago."

Paul: Had you seen them there before?"

Randy: "No sir. Am I in trouble?"

Paul: "Not so far, Randy. Who else knows about this?"

Randy: "No one."

Paul: Have you talked to your Dad about taking them?"

Randy: "No sir. He would beat me if he knew."

Paul: "Could anyone else have put them in his nightstand?"

Randy: "Not that I know of, he makes us stay clear of his room and we usually do."

Paul: "Are you trying to protect anyone by lying to me?"

Randy: "I'm not lying."

Paul: "Does your father know the rings are no longer in his nightstand drawer?"

Randy: "He's never said anything to me if he does."

Paul: "Ruby, I believe that is about all. Would you bring him back for more questions to help us if we need to ask more? We will try to be brief then as well."

Ruby: "I will".

Paul: It is very important that Raymond not be made aware of our questions, you know, for Randy's benefit. Let's keep this to ourselves, ok?"

Ruby: I will see to that and I know Randy will, but I hope they "are" stolen_and ya'll can nail the son of a bitch," she added, the hatred for her spouse coming out. Something about Hell having no fury like a woman scorned came to Paul's mind.

Paul: "That will be all, I will call you, Mrs. Butler if we need anything else."

As Mother and Son left and proceeded to their car, Paul and Joel began to discuss their next move which involved a lot of press, and a big show when they picked up Raymond for questioning. They had waited over a year for this moment and would make the most of it. From that minute forward, they made the often made mistake prosecutors make. The case was no longer an investigation but from that point forward was a prosecution of Raymond Butler and they focused on finding evidence that would convict him of capital murder of two young girls and maybe even three, never considering that he might be innocent. They could almost smell the gas themselves and could surely see the headlines.

CHAPTER 8

"I need to talk to my boss, of course, referring to DA Landon Fall, but I'm thinking we need a press conference announcing that we have brought in a person of interest or a suspect in connection with the Interstate murders of two young women from a year ago, "Paul suggested. "We need the sheriff and all the deputies and detectives he can spare for that little show of force," he added. "Depending on what the boss says, I suggest it be held on the courthouse steps, the day we bring him in for questioning and certainly no later than the day after". Joel, not to be left out, suggested "a small army of armed deputies and perhaps our S.W.A.T. team to make the arrest, along with the sheriff himself. I know L B will want in on the scene. Maybe take him into custody at his job, Trunkline Gas Company, during his day shift so we will have a full slate of employees witness it so they can spread the word. If not, I guess we are stuck with his home and only the tv station in Greenwood to cover it." "Wherever and whenever he's taken into custody, we need to coordinate with the tv station," Paul observed. He and Joel both agreed that this would be the first step in convicting Raymond. Convict him before trial in the eyes of the public. Forget the Constitution and the fact that innocence is prewued. Put the burden on him to prove he is not guilty. The rest will then come easy.

Both men then went their separate ways to talk to their respective bosses to inform them of the good news and get their direction on how to proceed from there. When Paul found Landon, he was not in his office, but on the way to play golf at the Cleveland Country Club. They talked by radio and agreed to meet at Landon's office at 3 o'clock that afternoon. He held off on telling Landon any specifics and only told him he wanted to update him on the Interstate murders. Paul signed off the radio and then called Joel at the sheriff's office to see if he and the sheriff could meet with them at that time as well. When Joel confirmed the meeting, Paul headed out to the Varsity Grill near Delta State to get a pizza for lunch, but his mind just really wasn't on food at the time. Like most people, particularly Southerners, eating was a force of habit and rarely the result of hunger.

It seemed as though 3 o'clock would never arrive but when it did, Paul was sitting in front of the DA's office when the sheriff with James Joel in tow showed up. Landon was inside waiting on all of them. They all went inside and after being offered and accepting coffee and soft drinks, they got down to business with Paul taking the lead and explaining to Landon and L B what they had discovered from talking with Randy Butler and David Perry at the pawn shop. He then told Landon and L B how he and Joel thought they should proceed from there. They were not surprised that the sheriff was all in on the plan but was somewhat taken aback by Landon's reluctance initially. "Let's look at the whole picture, guys. We have no direct evidence but all circumstantial," Landon pointed out. "Our whole case at this time is built on a fifteen year old kid's testimony linking the rings taken at the scene to his father, a statement that might prove to be prophetic in the days to come. I think we need more," he added. "Still no motive and we don't even know if he had the opportunity because he often worked nights. "Let's check on those things before we pull the trigger." The sheriff, always eager to go after the bad guy regardless of the case's weaknesses, argued the time to move was now. Joel agreed with his boss, interjecting that he would get a confession if they brought him in, but Landon stood steadfast. However, when Paul told him of the recent Sunflower County murder of Jennifer Garrett and its similarities to Interstate, Landon feared the public if this was the same killer and a fourth victim should the killer strike yet again, would be catastrophic for he and the sheriff politically. "Ok, take two days maximum and check out Butler's co-workers to see his shift for each murder without disclosing why you're asking. See what their opinion of him is. Does he have a violent temper, know either or both victims? Those sorts of things. That will give us time to set up the press and coordinate with WABG television in Greenwood and all local press outlets." Landon agreed.

Everyone nodded in agreement and the meeting ended and everyone headed out to work.

CHAPTER 9

aul drove the next morning out to Interstate where the Trunkline Gas Company compressor plant was located arriving about nine o'clock, an hour after shift change. He walked into the Superintendent's office and introduced himself to Devo Tatum, the superintendent of that plant. He asked general questions at first, such as how many total employees they had presently as compared to a year ago. How many they had on each shift and then asked for the work schedules of all employees over the last year. Tatum was glad to oblige and had his clerk furnish Paul with the records he needed. At 10 o'clock, the employees started pouring into the break room for their morning break and Paul was allowed to stay and mingle with them. He figured out quick who the clowns were, who was super serious and who the jackasses were as well. The biggest member of the latter class so far as he could tell based on the opinion of the other employees was clearly Raymond Butler. He was a 20-Year employee but had been barely promoted at all, satisfied to keep to himself and hardly socialized with anyone. When he spoke at all, it was sarcastic and demeaning to the others. His recent marital problems had left him even more caustic. He was opinionated, always believed himself to be right, whatever the situation. His only attempt at humor was to tell derogatory and demeaning jokes about women or disgusting jokes about perverted sex. One employee offered that he got this from reading hard core porn magazines he kept in his locker. He had shown the guys some of the most perverted sex acts ever imagined from those magazines. Sado-masochistic sex acts, animal sex and even torture and rape. For 1970 this type of porn was virtually unheard of unless you happen to be in New York, Los Angeles or Tijuana. Where Raymond got the porn, nobody knew. When Paul headed back to his office in Cleveland, he thought he had motive for Raymond, now if he only had opportunity. He'd find out soon enough when he studied the work schedules he had been provided.

CHAPTER 10

Paul sat at his desk under the air conditioning as opposed to the oppressive heat of the outside and went over the work schedules of Raymond Butler on the nights of each of the Interstate murders. He quickly discovered that on both cases Raymond was working day shift from 8:00 a.m. to 4:30 p.m. which meant he was off at night and free to commit the murders if he desired. There would be no alibi unless Raymond could concoct one on his own, or if his wife could provide one, but that wasn't likely given their current marital situation. Gleefully, he put a call in to DA Landon Fall to tell him the news. He surmised and related to Landon that he had discovered their suspect had motive in that he was a sexual pervert who was infatuated with perverted sex acts which included sado-masochism and bodily injury and/or rape, sometimes even post mortem. He had opportunity in that he was off work during both murders in Interstate. All that was needed now was a confession on his part since his possession of the rings taken in each murder was tied to him through his son. Though he conceded that the case was not air tight, it was so much more than they had ever had before. "Just for kicks, let's see what his shift was on the night of the recent murder of Jennifer Garrett," Landon suggested. "Already ahead of you, Paul replied. He was taking vacation days the day before and the day of the murder, so he's available to commit that one as well".

"Pick him up," Landon immediately said, "and see if he has an alibi for any of them. "Great!", responded Paul, "I'll notify the press." "Would you set up a press conference for a couple days away?", he added. "Gladly," Landon responded.

Paul's next step was to notify James Joel of the Bolivar County sheriff's office and arrange some deputies to accompany them to the Butler home to pick up Raymond. However, after talking to Joel, they both decided they could get more bang for the buck by making the arrest at Trunkline Gas, Raymond's place of employment. They had his work schedule so they knew when he would be there and would have a full shift of workers, as many as 25 to 30 fellow employees from across the county who would witness the arrest and spread the word that the Interstate Murderer had been arrested. They agreed to pick him up at 10 a.m. the day after tomorrow at the employees' usual break time. Joel promised Paul he would have at least eight armed deputies go with them in at least 3 squad cars, all with lights flashing and sirens sounding. They hung up from the call and started counting down the time to 10 a.m., some 36 hours away. Paul relayed the plans to Landon who was all in on it as well as to Sheriff L. B. Wilson who was, as he put it "tickled shitless". This day had been a long day coming for all of them. Despite their best efforts, they had hit one brick wall after the other, but their persistence was about to pay off it seemed.

"Can't wait to interrogate him," Joel said. "I'll break the bastard down." He'll be glad to confess before I'm through with him. "Wonder how the folks that live around him are gonna react when they hear the killer has been living in their midst the whole time. Those are close-knit friends and family out there," Paul wondered aloud. "You know how it always is", Joel replied. "Some of em will swear they figured it all along". "Others will defend him, but everybody will be glad we got the son of a bitch, especially if we are able to pin the Garrett murder on him as well." "Damn right they will", Paul agreed. "I was going to let the Sunflower County DA know about this, but I'll wait until after we pick Butler up to do so. Don't think it would leak from them, but no use taking a chance on it either. "I can hardly wait to go get him," Paul added. Both Paul and Joel headed out to The Thicket, a local bar and grill just outside of town that both had frequented all too many times for a well deserved beer at the end of a successful day. The first beer was so good, they decided another was in order. After it, they had one more to wash down a plate of fried catfish, hushpuppies and cole slaw.

CHAPTER 11

At the previously arranged time a day later, Paul arrived at the Bolivar courthouse in Cleveland and met up with Joel and nine other deputies in four other squad cars and together they started the 20 minute drive from Cleveland out to Trunkline Gas Company in Interstate. All squad cars had bar lights flashing and sirens squealing. Paul's car, an unmarked Ford with a blue lights flashing from the dash, led the way. As a practical matter, the lights and sirens were not necessary, but they sent the word to the general public that the Law was out and about and something huge was going down. Just the message they wanted to send. Joel and Paul rode together leading the caravan and talked as they went.

I've been watching the national news lately and a few cases out in California caught my attention and reminded me of this one. "One is where a movie star's home was targeted by someone and everyone there was killed. Star's name was Sharon Tate and she was pregnant as well. Then two nights later, another couple was killed in the Los Angeles area," he told Paul. "These murders were noteworthy and reminded me of our cases in that there was no obvious motive. Doesn't appear to be a robbery gone bad, just a gruesome killing of about seven people in two nights, both home invasions resulting in murder. But a lot of clues were left like bloody handprints, fingerprints and other physical evidence." "They'll have an easier time than us solving that one", he went on. "The one I heard about that most resembles ours concerns multiple murders in the San Francisco Bay area where someone has killed a number of teenagers parking on Lover's Lanes in that area. No motives or connections to the victims, they just a happened to be in the wrong place at the wrong time," Joel continued to describe. "The animal calls himself Zodiac. Very similar to our cases from the looks of it at this time in that somebody is killing for the sake of killing, except Zodiac is apparently sending clues through the newspaper to the police. He's obviously not as smart as Raymond Butler so far, Joel further described, adding "I think the world has gone crazy."

"I've been reading up on those that commit multiple murders and what psychologists think make them tick," Paul chimed. "Fascinating stuff, actually. Some think it is sex driven, which sounds like Raymond Butler. Others think it is triggered by the moon phases." He had no way of knowing, but the upcoming decade of the 70s would see those who commit multiple murders greatly expand beyond anything anyone could imagine before and they would gain great notoriety. From the mass murders of Charles Manson's followers only a year before to serial killings by such notorious murderers in the 70s such as Ted Bundy, Son of Sam killer David Berkowitz and John Wayne Gacy. Berkowitz, Bundy and Gacy would fit the profile of Raymond Butler more than they would have liked: All four would murder over a period of days or months, all but Berkowitz would involve sex with their victims. Their victims were largely strangers before they were killed and none had any apparent motive other than a lust for killing and that fact alone was enough to chill the blood of anybody.

As they neared the Trunkline compressor station, Paul radioed to all the units there to proceed behind his car and exit when he did with shotguns in tow along with their handguns on their side. One deputy was directed to bring a bullet proof vest for Raymond to wear after the arrest to prevent any harm from coming to him from angered onlookers, although there would be no way for anyone to know except his fellow employees that he had been working alongside all morning why he was being taken into custody. However, it made for a Good show and revealed to the public how serious Raymond's charge must be and how heinous his crime was, again, all part of the show. As the caravan entered the gates of the station, lights flashing and sirens wailing, they all pulled to a stop outside the Plant office and all eleven men exited with their weapons drawn and Paul leading the way. The WABG TV news van was already there as agreed with cameras rolling. Once all were inside, Paul demanded that the superintendent, Devo Tatum, bring Raymond Butler to the office. He obliged without question and Raymond was dispatched there, arriving within a few minutes to the glaring television camera lights. When he walked in, Paul and Joel both approached him and Paul said, for the benefit of the camera mostly, "Are you Raymond Butler?", knowing that he was. When he said in the affirmative, He was grabbed by Joel who spun him around and brought both hands behind him in order to cuff him as Paul informed him, "You are being taken into custody at this time for questioning in the matter of the murders of Linda Strawberry and Janice Galtelli. You have the right to remain silent and the right to an attorney and if you cannot afford one, an attorney will be appointed for you at the expense of Bolivar County. If you give up the right to remain silent, anything you say can and will be used against you in a court of law. Do you understand these rights as I have explained them to you?" Paul clearly and deliberately told him and the general public through the camera. Paul nodded his affirmance and he was immediately uncuffed while the vest was placed on him and then the cuffs put back on him, all the while being whisked out the door to Paul's waiting Ford. Though the reporter with the cameraman shouted a couple of questions about the arrest, Paul declined comment at this time, assuring him there would be a full press conference very soon and all questions would be answered there to the extent that they could. The performance complete, all officers returned to their cars and headed in a caravan back to the Bolivar County courthouse and sheriff's office with its waiting jail cell. "I want to know what this is all about, "Raymond asked Paul and Joel over and over. "I ain't done a damn thing and anybody that says I have, is a damn liar. You hear me?" Joel assured him they would talk when they got to the sheriff's office, but he needed to shut up for the time being. As they left the plant grounds, Paul saw a crowd of bewildered employees outside the office in his rear view mirror. They had done all they had set out to do and he was pleased.

When the caravan arrived at the sheriff's office, Paul parked and he and Joel helped Raymond out of the back seat, still in the vest and cuffed, walked him up the steps of the SO and into an interrogation room with a reel to reel recorder on the desk with two chairs in front of the desk and one behind. They seated Raymond in the single chair behind the desk and Paul and Joel sat in front. "Now tell me what the hell is going on", Raymond demanded. "And take these damn cuffs off of me."

Joel thought to himself, "I have only been around him about 45 minutes total and I already can't stand the son of a bitch."

"You want to ask the questions or do you want me to?", Paul asked Joel. "Let me go ahead and start," he added before Joel could answer. The date is September 23, 1970, and we are here in the interrogation room at the Bolivar County Sheriff's office. The time is approximately 11:50 a.m. and present are Detective James Joel of the Bolivar SO, Paul Lane of the District Attorney's office and Raymond Butler. Does anybody disagree with anything I've said at his time?" No one disagreed so Paul reluctantly turned the questioning over to over to Joel.

Joel: Raymond, I'm James Joel, chief deputy with the Bolivar sheriff's office. You are Raymond Butler that lives down in Interstate Woods in the southeast part of the county, are you not?"

Raymond: I am. Lived there for 20 years or so.

Joel: Have you heard of the murders of Linda Strawberry and Janice Galelli down in that community a little over a year ago?

Raymond: I've heard of em, yes. It was talk of the community at the time, but that's all I know about em. Just that they were killed in their homes according to the tv and the newspaper. Same thing everybody else knows. Ya'll are batshit crazy if you think I had anything to do with them, I'll tell you that right now.

Joel: Did you know either of the girls, personally?

RAYMOND: I knew the Strawberry girl and her family. They went to the Interstate Baptist Church, same as me, but they were more active in it than me. I considered myself friends with her Daddy. He was a deacon there. She sang solos in church sometimes.

JOEL: How about Janice Galtelli, did you know her?

RAYMOND: Never saw her before in my life and don't know nothing about her. Shame for both of them getting killed. He was desperately looking for some way to show he cared without showing he was that interested or concerned.

JOEL asked, "Can you tell me where you were or what you were doing, Raymond, specifically on August 4, 1969 and the week thereafter?" "Hell no, do you know where you were on the night of July 16, 1970?" Raymond responded smugly.

JOEL: Actually, I do, because that just happens to be my anniversary and I took my wife to dinner at the Venetian Restaurant in Greenville that night.

RAYMOND: Well, I ain't got no idea where I was, but it sure as hell wasn't out with my old lady. When can I get something to eat?

Paul was satisfied because Raymond was now stuck with the answer that he didn't know where he was and accordingly couldn't later come up with an alibi.

JOEL: It may be a little while depending on how cooperative you are here. You like looking at porn mags don't you, Raymond?

RAYMOND: Same as any man, I guess.

Joel: You like the kinky stuff, though don't you, like sex with torture, humiliation and rough role playing?

RAYMOND: Where you getting this from? From Ruby? I swear before God anything we ever did in bed, she instigated and liked it. Rape role play, tying up, she loved it all.

JOEL; You need to understand right now Raymond, we believe we have your ass. You were pretty careful on those nights, but not as careful as you thought. You left something behind and we can track it right to you. You may sniff gas at Parchman, Raymond. It's all up to you. Help us now and we'll try to help you, but this is your one shot to help yourself. After this, we go for the whole enchilada. The least you're looking at is life without parole, if you're lucky. We will put you in Parchman Farm with the rest of the scum of the earth and you can say goodbye to your family, your job, your house and everything else. Your worst nightmare is about to come true. Maybe them kids can come see you on death row. You know we're serious or we wouldn't have made such a scene today if we had any doubt. Help yourself, Raymond, now or never.

RAYMOND: Can I at least have some water? And a lawyer? I'm dying here.

JOEL: Don't want you to die here, Raymond. Save it for the gas chamber.

CHAPTER 12

When Raymond asked for a lawyer, Paul and Joel knew the interrogation had to stop or they risked the entire statement being excluded from evidence and they were happy with what they had. It wasn't a confession, but he had admitted to deviant sexual practices that mimicked the crime scenes in both murders. And they had planted the seed of conviction which just might get them a plea deal to life without parole if the victims' family agreed. What few people knew, especially Raymond was that executions across the United States might soon be stayed by the US Supreme Court and nobody knew when or if they would resume. Only time would tell. They uncuffed Raymond and walked him to a cell, took off his bullet proof vest and locked him up. When he asked about bond, they told him he was being held without bond but one might eventually be set. They allowed him a phone call and he used it to call Jackson Jones a local divorce attorney who practiced some criminal law but mainly was a ham and egger lawyer, one that handled a little of everything in order to earn a living. Raymond had earlier retained him to represent him in the divorce that Ruby filed and thought he might get a discount from him for this case. It's sad to think that some people look for bargain basement lawyers even when their ass is on the line, but it is true more often than not. He and Jones came to a financial agreement over the phone and Raymond assured him he would get the $5,000.00 retainer for him as soon as he could liquidate his retirement funds that Trunkline held. Meanwhile, Joel and Paul were on their way to The Thicket bar and grill for beers and sandwiches in celebration of their accomplishments of the day. They wanted to get back by 5:00 p.m. in order to catch themselves on the Channel 6 News.

CHAPTER 13

As it turned out, there was no need to rush home for the news. The bar had a television set going and it was tuned to channel six so everybody could see the news covering the big arrest earlier in the day. Everyone around them were backslapping Joel and Paul and calling them movie stars as well as congratulating them on bringing the long opened case to its conclusion. Someone even bought them a couple of beers each afterwards. The two ate their ham and cheese sandwiches and washed them down with beers and afterwards were ready to call it a night and head home. It was the most productive day they had experienced in a long time. Before they left, Paul used the bar's phone to call Landon at home and arrange an 8:00 a.m. meeting in his office in the morning to bring him up to speed on what they had learned from Raymond. He promised to bring doughnuts for them all from the Delta Cream Donut Shop when he came in the morning.

At exactly 8:00 a.m., Paul strode into Landon's office with a couple dozen of assorted doughnuts in tow. Landon was leaned back in his high-backed office chair waiting when Paul came in and sat across the desk from him. Landon's secretary brought coffee in for herself and Landon along with a cold coke from the office refrigerator for Paul.

"Talk to me," Landon barked, and Paul began to relay the events of the day before as he recalled them. "I believe the biggest thing is that Raymond acknowledges having rough sex with his wife, which plays into our theory of motive," Paul surmised. "No confession and nothing but denials, unfortunately, he added, but when we question Ruby, his wife, we might find some rape role playing, etc., that would strengthen our motive case". "Whether it counts right now or not, I assure you the whole county is convinced of his guilt", Raymond predicted. "That will help with public perception of the job we're doing which is good, especially if it turns out this Garrett murder in Sunflower County is related to ours," Landon agreed. Paul was always impressed with the way Landon always looked at the political perspective in any scenario.

"Oh, and Raymond has retained Jackson Jones to represent him on this, same lawyer he had representing him in his divorce," said Paul. "Hope he wears the same tan corduroy coat he wears every day to the trial when we set it," Landon laughed. "That'll impress the jury." "What's our next move, boss?" Paul asked. "I would like to hear what his wife has to say", Landon answered. "We've got plenty already for an indictment, especially as long as the kid sticks to his story about the rings". Let's get the grand jury report ready, get the indictment next month when the grand jury meets and head to trial. Twenty bucks says it never goes to trial, but Jones instead pleads him to life," Landon wagered. "May very well be the case, Paul reluctantly agreed, However, for the victims' sake and our sake as public servants who would like to stay in office, we will need the victims' families' permission to make that type of plea offer." "Damn right", agreed Landon. The conversation eventually went from a murder case to the subject of football and the season the Ole Miss Rebels were having over in Oxford. Strangely enough, no one ever talked about Delta State's team even though they were located in Cleveland, probably due to the fact that they were Division II as opposed to the big boys in Division I like the Rebels, the Mississippi State Bulldogs, LSU or

Alabama. The gathering finally broke up with everyone voicing their opinion as to the record their team would have in December when the season was finally over. It was really amazing how people in the South put more emphasis on College football than anything else, even capital murder.

CHAPTER 14

At Shaw High School, on Monday morning following the arrest of Raymond Butler on two counts of capital murder, Mrs. Ferretti looked to the back corner of her home room class and watched Randy Butler. Like everyone, she had heard the news over the weekend and wondered how Randy would react. Surprisingly, he was quiet and withdrawn and upon closer look, had his head down on his desk, apparently crying to himself. She didn't know if the other kids had been cruel to him as they often can be, or if the stress of the situation was working on him, if not both. Either way, she walked to the back of the class, put her arm around him and got him to get up and go outside the classroom with her. They walked down the hall to the empty classroom next door, their footsteps clopping on the oak hardwood floor of the hall, went inside the empty room and sat down at the empty teacher's desk, she on the backside with Randy in a chair in front. Mrs. Ferretti did her best to console him without too much fuss. She told him she understood it was a bad time for him and offered to help in any way that she could, all he needed to do was ask her. She felt sorry for him beyond measure. He had had a miserable home life thus far: Mother and father divorcing, an alcoholic father who had physically abused him at times, and a mother who really didn't want him but preferred to drown her problems much the way his father did. Now there was a better than even chance that his father would go to prison or worse, to death row. You just don't understand, Mrs. Ferretti, I'm the reason my father is in this jam. "I know, Randy", she responded, believing he was blaming himself for having to point the finger at his father because he had found the rings in his father's nightstand as he told the police. "You don't know the half of it", Randy tearfully said. He couldn't believe a little white lie that he told had gotten things so screwed up, yet it had. "Would you like to drink a coke?", Mr. Ferretti inquired. It seemed like drinking a coke always made anybody feel better about anything. After he nodded, she went down to the teachers' lounge and got a coke from the machine and brought it back for him. She gave him time to drink it and they returned to her home room classroom together. As Randy took his seat in the back he whispered to his friend Wesley across the aisle. "We gotta talk at recess," he whispered to his pal. "I got some decisions to make", Randy added. Neither of the boys were in the mood to listen to any geography lecture after that. They both watched the large round-faced clock on the wall above the teacher's desk continuously, hoping recess at 9:30 a.m. would hurry up and get there. When the bell finally rang, the class emptied and Randy and Weasel made a mad dash to the front steps of the school and sat on the landing where the huge decorative concrete balls sat.

"How's your old man?" Weasel asked. Don't really know, he's still in jail, no bond," Randy replied. Mom says they will set his bond today, most likely and if he can make it, he'll get out and be home, Randy added." "Good!" said Weasel. "I don't know if it is or not," chimed Randy. "He's gonna beat the hell out of me for what I said". "What exactly did you say, Randy", Weasel inquired. "I told the pawnshop man that I found the rings in Dad's nightstand. Then I told the Law the same thing under oath when they questioned me about it., Randy answered. "I couldn't change my story then after telling it before. I had no idea they had been taken from a murder scene. I just didn't want it known that I stole from the church," he explained.

"I told ya they was poison didn't I", Weasel reminded Randy. "Yeah, ya did, Randy conceded, but that's ancient history now." "What am I gonna do now?" Randy pleaded, while looking at Weasel as if some divine answer would come to him. "If you tell the truth now, they'll prosecute you for lying under oath, for perjury and theft and probably send you to jail. Maybe even charge you with those murders." Weasel opined, all those hours of watching **Adam 12**, **Dragnet** and **Highway Patrol** finally paying off. Randy felt sick at his stomach, but fortunately the bell rang and the two had to hurry back to class.

Randy couldn't concentrate on anything else in class except the fix he had gotten his life into at the moment. He wanted to get out of school and head home, but he thought his Dad might be waiting on him and if not, his Mom would certainly be there to question him, so that was just as bad. He was miserable and had no one to blame but his own greedy self. At lunchtime in the school cafeteria, Randy and Weasel sat by themselves away from their other friends and munched on sloppy Joes and a peanut butter cookie. That happened to be Randy's lunchroom favorite, but not surprisingly, today they had very little taste to him.

CHAPTER 15

Back in Cleveland, attorney Jackson Jones entered the sheriff's office and asked to see his client, Raymond Butler. He was summarily escorted down the row of cells where his client was kept and then both attorney and client were escorted to a room reserved for such consultation visits.

"Let me get straight to the point, Raymond," Jones told him. "Are you guilty of the murders you are suspected of committing? You understand about Attorney-client privilege, don't you?" the lawyer asked his client. "Yes, I do and hell no, I ain't done nothing they say I have," Raymond responded. "Well, the investigation report the DA's office let me see says you had a ring taken from the scene of each murder found in your nightstand drawer by your son who tried to hock them," Jones answered. "How do you explain that?" "I never seen em, maybe that boy of mine killed em for all I know. He's a liar at best," responded Raymond. "We won't get very far just denying it and then accusing your fifteen year old son of committing multiple murders," Jones warned. "That's the only explanation I know of, anyway", Raymond retorted.

"Let's talk about my fee," Jones said. "I'm going to need $20,000.00 up front and will charge $75.00 per hour from and after that, payable in full before we go to trial. Will you be able to get that kind of money out of your retirement at Trunkline, Raymond? I'm already working to get you a bond set if I can," Jones added.

"I got to get out of here to do anything," Raymond said in frustration. "DA says they can't agree to less than $500,000.00 if any", was his lawyer's response. How much will I have to come up with, Raymond asked immediately. Bond agent can write that for 10% or $50,000, was the dreaded answer from his lawyer," None of it refundable."

"So, I got to come up with $70,000.00 to start with?" Raymond asked. I don't have that much in retirement, savings and everything else, so far as I know, but I'll get what I can", Raymond stated. Can you call Devo Tatum out at Trunkline for me to get things started?" he further asked. "I will. I'll see if he can get me the paperwork to bring to you", Jones assured him.

Jones left Raymond at the jail and headed back to his office to call Tatum, already thinking of the bills he could pay with that $20,000.00. He then called the DA who assured him he would agree to the Circuit Judge setting a half million dollar bond as previously suggested, if the victims' family agreed. Jones didn't have a warm and fuzzy feeling about his client's innocence at the moment, but it was really too early to tell as if it really mattered. He was under a legal obligation to give him his best representation either way. It's no wonder people hated lawyers, he thought.

Back at the jail, Raymond Paced back and forth in his small cell like a caged animal, lamenting his situation. A couple days ago his biggest worry was how much his wife would take from him in the divorce. Now he was in jail, bankrupt for all practical purposes and thought a mass murder by people he had grown up with, not to mention he had a son that obviously hated him so much he was willing to falsely send him to the gas chamber at Parchman prison. He looked at his cot and the sheet covering it and looked up to a vent at the top of his cell. He could tie one end of the sheet to that vent, the other around his neck and hang himself if he sank any lower in depression. At the moment that seemed attractive to him, but he would wait a bit and see if he could wake up from this nightmare, but in his mind, he knew there was always that option if it got too bad for him. Frankly, at the present time, he couldn't imagine how it could get worse, but he would try to see it through at least for a few days.

Ruby Butler was buying groceries at the Piggly Wiggly grocery store in Shaw. Every time she looked up from the shelves, she felt people staring at her. She knew they were thinking, how she could have lived with a monster like Raymond Butler for the last year after he murdered those young girls. She thought they must also wonder if she knew about it, especially since she had separated from him and filed for divorce on the grounds of habitual cruel and inhuman treatment, a catch all ground most people used to get a divorce since Mississippi had no irreconcilable differences ground that could be used just yet. She knew they were talking about her and she best get used to it, but she wanted that divorce as soon as she could get it. The thought of seeing him or having him touch her, even in a non-sexual way made her skin crawl. She checked out, had the young bag boy put the groceries in her car and headed to her rented apartment in Cleveland, stopping by the Sandpit Store on the way. It was about 4:00 p.m. and some of the regulars were there throwing back a beer on their way home from work and she really needed one herself. She felt glaring and staring eyes as she entered, but she knew these people pretty well and felt a little more comfortable than earlier at the grocery store. That was, until she saw Mrs. Peggy Butler, Raymond's mother standing at the end of the counter. She had dreaded this meeting, but it was best to get it over with sooner than later. "HI, Ruby," Mrs. Butler said politely. Ruby responded politely as well, "HI Peggy, good to see you." Peggy walked up to her, gently pulled her by the arm a few steps away from everyone else and whispered to her, "Just please tell me you didn't put Randy up to framing Raymond like this." "I most certainly did not," Ruby said. "I'm probably more shocked than you about the whole mess." "How much do you want in cash to settle the divorce and tell Randy to not make those accusations anymore," Peggy asked. Ruby's attention was strictly on Peggy's offer and she was more than curious. "I have told my lawyer, John Marshall, that I would settle with Raymond for half of his retirement with Trunkline which I think is worth about $60,000.00 and a deed to the house free and clear of any debts on it. I'll pay my credit card and he can pay his. I want my car and he can keep his. Get me that and I'll talk to Randy and tell him to make sure he is telling the truth, but that's all I can do with him." "Done deal, Peggy responded. I'll get the money and talk to Raymond and his lawyer". "One other stipulation, I want this done within a week, the divorce final and all. I'm already sick of people staring at me because of him. I'm sure he wants the same thing," Peggy replied. They actually hugged and Ruby headed out the door to go home, then remembered she had not paid for her beer, but she was no longer interested in hanging out with this crowd, so she went back in, paid and quickly left.

CHAPTER 16

Randy was much like Ruby in that he thought everyone was staring and talking about him and probably were. Everyone in the county knew his father was a suspected murderer in the most notorious crime in the county in anyone's memory. Weasel didn't sit with him on the bus ride home and Randy was certain he was ashamed to be seen with him. Everyone within miles of his home knew that Randy's testimony had nailed his father to the wall and wondered if his testimony would ultimately send his father to death row at Parchman. That was a hell of a cross for a fifteen year old kid to carry, but it was Randy's to bear. He wished a thousand times he could turn back the clock and just throw the rings away and forget all this. Weasel had been right from the beginning. Those rings were toxic, like radioactive material and were poison to everyone that came into contact with them. For the foreseeable future, Randy just wanted to be alone, away from the world of lawyers, cops, family and even friends.

When the bus got to Randy's house, he was sick to see his mom's car in the drive. She could have got his dad out of jail and brought him home or at best was there to talk to him about the whole episode, neither scenario appealing to him in the least. He exited the bus and went inside to find his mother waiting on the couch. "Sit down, Randy and let's talk," she told him before he had a chance to say anything. "How was school?" "Not bad, he said and then followed up with, "for a kid that has a dad in jail for killing two girls and I'm the one who put him there." "You are the key to him being there for a fact!" she agreed. "Is there any doubt in your mind that his nightstand is where you found those rings? She queried. "No ma'am," he replied without any hesitation. He was forced to ride this lie from now on or face the legal and religious consequences of perjury and stealing from the church. Like a million other people in the world, he wanted so bad to turn back the hands of time.

"I want you to know the seriousness of your story that has been told to the police," she said. "It's not a story, Mom. It's the God's honest truth," he said, almost indignantly. He thought if he told the lie often enough, he might believe it himself and so would everybody else, much the same as Josef Goebbels had said in Nazi Germany some thirty years before. Either way, there was no turning back now. That was his story and he was sticking to it. "I know son, but your father is in jail and may be for a long, long time because of it. You understand, that don't you?" she said. "I know, Mom, I wish I had never told where I got em, but I had no idea they came from those murders," Randy said, crying into his hands. "It's okay, son, I just wanted to make sure you understand how serious this is," she told him, putting her arm around him. "I think we need to be in church this Sunday, I'll pick you up at 9:45 so we can be in Sunday School by 10:00 a.m. when it starts, then we'll stay for Brother Kirksey's sermon and then come home afterwards", his mother said as she lit another cigarette. The thought hit Randy basically for the first time at the mention of the pastor's name. If his dad was accused of murdering two girls because the police thought he had the rings in his possession, would they think the same of Pastor Kirksey if they knew what Randy really knew. Also, what was Brother Kirksey thinking now, because he knew the rings were taken from his desk. If he was a killer, Randy was sure he was happy his father was the one being accused, but if he feared Randy might come clean with the real truth, he might come after him to keep him quiet, he thought. The thought of a multiple killer wanting him dead or trying to get to him was terrifying. Now he had something else to worry about. Nothing seemed to be working out for Randy and he had no one to blame but himself. He had no idea how a small lie like he told could balloon into all this, but it had. It was impossible for anyone to understand the enormous psychological pressure on Randy. It just seemed the consequences far exceeded the sin. His mother talked a little more to him about school and church and then in a short while told him she had to go put groceries away at her apartment before her refrigerated goods spoiled in the heat of the Delta sun while sitting in her car. Besides, she wanted to try and call his father's lawyer and see what was expected next. She never bothered to ask if Randy wanted to go with her which was fine by him because he did not. She got up and left the house, leaving Randy to continue crying alone. He watched her spin out of the gravel driveway, then went into the kitchen where he discovered she had left a loaf of bread, some rag bologna and sliced hoop cheese sitting on the counter for his supper. It was far from his favorite, but at least he would have something. He started making the sandwiches when he saw the bag of Lay's *Ruffle* potato chips there. He picked up the phone and called his grandmother, Peggy, who lived less than a mile away just to check on his younger brother and sister. They had been with her since Raymond had been taken into custody. He had been invited to stay with her as well, but he was old enough to stay by himself, he thought, and so he had done so now for the past couple of weeks. It was close to sunset and that was bad, since for some reason, the ending of the day seemed to increase Randy's depression and concern.

CHAPTER 17

When Ruby got to her apartment back in Cleveland, she called Raymond's lawyer who quickly told her that he couldn't speak with her since she was represented by an attorney herself and advised her to have her attorney call him instead if she had something she needed to tell him. She called Her lawyer, John Marshall, and informed him of the conversation and purported settlement she had previously with Raymond's mother, Peggy. He assured her he would talk with him tomorrow and start the process of drafting the necessary paperwork to resolve the divorce under the terms Ruby and Peggy had agreed. As she hung up the phone, there was a knock at her door. When she answered it, she found Chief deputy James Joel there asking her to come to the sheriff's office to answer a few questions. She agreed and went with him in his squad car. When they went into the sheriff's office and was seated at the table, she saw that Paul Lane was also there as was the same reel to reel tape reorder that had been there when she and Randy had been there previously. Paul turned it on after they exchanged pleasantries and the preliminary information about the date and time as well as those present in the room which was dictated by Paul. The questioning began by Joel.

Joel: Has everything been correctly stated so far, Mrs. Butler?

Ruby: It has.

Joel: You have been sworn have you not?

Ruby: I have.

Joel: You currently have an attorney representing you, John Marshal, but he only represents you in your divorce against your husband and nothing else. Is that correct?

Ruby: That is correct.

Joel: I'm going to ask you some questions that may be embarrassing, but I must do so. If at any time you want me to stop questioning and have your attorney here, I will do so. Is that understood?

Ruby: It is, but I don't need him here costing me money.

Joel: I understand.

Joel: You are Ruby Butler, wife of Raymond Butler, is that right?

Ruby: Yes.

Joel: During your marriage to Raymond, when the two of you engaged in sex, would you describe Raymond as vanilla or kinky, or neither?

Ruby: Definitely kinky.

Joel: How so?

Ruby: He liked what I call angry sex, usually a little rough.

Joel: Give me some examples.

Ruby: Well, he liked to tie me up, blindfold me and slap me around before we did it, He would sometimes choke me with his hands or with my stockings. It scared me a lot at times.

Joel: Did he ever physically hurt you?

Ruby: Not really, but I almost passed out once from the choking and that seemed to rev him up even more.

The questioning went on for probably 20 minutes and then concluded. Both Joel and Paul apologized for the nature of the questions and prepared to leave. "If my lawyer wants a copy of that for my divorce, can he get it?" she asked as they all got up. "Absolutely," replied Joel and Paul in unison. "Just have him contact us". And with that, Joel drove her back to her apartment. Paul immediately called Landon to give him the good news. Ruby was now almost as important a witness as Randy was. However, it was Landon that doused the flames of excitement a little by reminding Paul that Mississippi law prohibited a spouse from testifying against his/her spouse except in cases against each other. Therefore, there was no problem with her or Raymond testifying against the other in the divorce, but they could not in the criminal action. It was incredibly important that the divorce be completed by the time the murder trial came up for hearing. Otherwise, Ruby, as Raymond's wife would not be able to testify as to Raymond's infatuation for choking as a prelude to sex. Which would assist in showing motive for the murders. No problem, thought Paul, he would get in touch with John Marshall and see if he could find out what the timeline on the divorce was. In the meantime, he would keep Ruby's status as a possible witness close to his chest. If Raymond wanted to use her as a witness for himself in the criminal trial for whatever reason he was free to waive the privilege and use her, but she could not testify against him on behalf of the prosecution as long as they were married.

CHAPTER 18

True to her word, Ruby arrived the following Sunday on time to pick Randy up to go to church and Sunday School at the Interstate Baptist Church. Randy had dreaded this because it would be the first time he and Pastor Kirksey had seen each other and only the Pastor and God Almighty knew the truth about the rings. That, not withstanding, this would be the first church service for the membership since one of their own had been arrested and charged with the infamous Interstate murders and was sure to be a hot topic. Add to all of that that a joint press conference between the district attorney's office and the Bolivar County Sheriff's Office was scheduled for the next day at 4:00 pm in front of the county courthouse and the news was truly the talk of the community, county and the Mississippi Delta. The church seemed to be at full capacity on this day and everyone huddled in small groups before going to their respective Sunday school rooms.

When Randy walked into his Sunday school class, he felt like all eyes were on him and they no doubt were. Some kids stared at him while others refused to make eye contact, both managing to make him feel awkward. He forced himself to listen to Mrs. King's lesson at least until Pastor WD Kirksey stuck his head into the room, looked directly at him and said "Randy Butler, before you leave after service, would you come to my study, please sir? I need to have a little chat with you." Randy was a basket case from then forward, unable to concentrate about anything but the pending meeting with the Pastor, the man who at the least knew Randy was a liar and a thief and also knew the pastor could be a killer. His mouth was dry, his heart was racing and he gave some serious thought to running out and avoiding the confrontation all together but decided it was probably happening sooner or later and was accordingly best to get it over today. Surely, he was safe here in church with this many witnesses present, he thought. When Sunday school was over and the service began he couldn't wait for it all to be over. However, as is usually the case in such situations, the service seemed never ending.

"If you have your Bibles, please turn to Deuteronomy Chapter 5, beginning with verse 1:" and then, reading he continued, "Hear O Israel, the statutes and judgements which I speak in your ears this day, that you may learn them, and keep, and do them". His voice roared and then went soft and then began roaring again as he began to quote the Ten Commandments as given to Israel by God through Moses. Randy heard them all, but a few reverberated through his mind, "Honour thy father and thy mother," "Thou shalt not steal", "Neither shall thy bear false witness against thy neighbor" He was certain the pastor was speaking directly to him and he expected the mighty hand of God to grab him by his collar at any second. As the pastor wrapped up his sermon, he quoted from Deuteronomy 5:9: For I the Lord thy God am a jealous God, visiting the iniquity of the Fathers upon the children unto the third and fourth generation of them that hate me. He knew Kirksey was talking directly to him as a scare tactic and to the flock in general to assure them that God would punish both the father murderer and his son and grandchildren for what he had done. It worked with Randy because it unnerved him as he sat and listened.

When the service was over, he reluctantly went to the pastor's study, a place he had not visited since taking the rings and plopped down in a chair on the opposite side of the desk from the pastor's high back chair. He didn't have to wait long before the preacher came in, greeted him with a handshake and sat down at his desk. "Randy, it seems you have become the star in a story involving your father, have you not?" Kirksey asked him. "I guess I have," Randy responded. "The most important thing you need to know and remember, is that once you have told this story to the police you should never waiver from it. To say otherwise would cause you serious legal problems and charges that would affect you for the rest of your life. You could be charged with accessory to murder after the fact, perjury, grand larceny or conspiracy to commit either of those", he told Randy as if he was his lawyer. "More importantly, depending on how you changed your story, your life could be in danger," he preached to Randy. "You understand that?" He asked Randy. Randy heard him loud and clear, especially the part about his life being in danger depending on what he told differently than what he had already said. The preacher was letting him know in no uncertain terms that he would come for him if he was accused by him. Randy felt nauseous and started to get up from his chair. "Before you go", Kirksey warned, "I want to know that we understand each other completely and you know how serious this is". "I do", Randy replied and went for the door where he saw his mother standing just outside and went immediately to the car with her and left. He was visibly shaken, but he didn't think his mother noticed and was glad to get back home a few minutes later. His mother left to go back to Cleveland and Randy was actually relieved to be alone.

CHAPTER 19

The next afternoon shortly before 4:00 p.m., a crowd began to gather on the south side of the Bolivar County courthouse in Cleveland. A large contingent of law enforcement officers from the sheriff's department, the District Attorney, Landon Fall, Paul Lane and Sheriff L.B. Wilson stood behind a bank of microphones supplied by WABG-TV in nearby Greenwood, Mississippi., a host of reporters from ***The Bolivar Commercial***, ***The Delta Democrat Times***, ***The Greenwood Commonwealth***, ***The Clarion Ledger***, the Memphis, Tennessee ***Commercial Appeal*** and other newspapers from across the Delta as well as the state assembled in front of the microphones with tape recorders, cameras and notepads, while a throng of citizens from around the county filled the yard behind them, anxious to learn something about the infamous case. Landon Fall began at precisely 4:00 p.m. by welcoming both press and citizens to the press conference and then introducing Paul Lane who would read a statement. Paul stepped up to the mic, cleared his throat and read the following statement:

A few days ago, following an investigation by the Bolivar County Sheriff's office and the district attorney's office for the 11th Circuit District,

Raymond Butler, age 49, who resides at 623 Trunkline Road in the Interstate Community was taken into custody and charged with the murders of Linda Strawberry and Janice Galtelli last year, both residents of Interstate. He was taken into custody without incident at his place of employment, Trunkline Gas Company following a tip from a local business who received property apparently taken from the scene of both murders. This proves that law enforcement can be more effective when assisted by its citizens, and we thank Perry's Pawn and Used Cars for their help. I'll be happy to respond to any questions I can at this time.

"What bond has been set for Mr. Butler?" asked the reporter for WABG. Paul replied, "He is currently being held without bond due to the heinous nature of the crimes. "However, a bond hearing will be held after indictment and I anticipate a sizable bond will be set under the Supreme Court guidelines", Paul added. "How much do you anticipate and when will the indictment come down?" asked ***The Commercial Appeal*** reporter. "We would talk to the families of the victims and see what they would be comfortable with initially, and I anticipate presenting the case to the Bolivar County Grand Jury early next week. I would not speculate on the amount requested until after speaking to the victims' family", Paul answered. "Has he given a confession?" Asked the reporter from ***The Bolivar Commercial***. Paul replied, "No he has not, but has been questioned previously." "We are no longer able to question him since he has retained local attorney Jackson Jones." Paul added. "What property that you referred to in your statement connects him to the crime?" asked ***The Clarion Ledger*** reporter. "I believe that will have to wait until trial to be revealed so as not to jeopardize the prosecution," Paul responded. "Are there any plea negotiations ongoing?" asked the reporter representing **The Delta Democrat Times**. "There are not," responded Landon Fall. "Do you anticipate any?" asked **The Greenwood Commonwealth**. "Only after consultation with the families of the victims," replied Landon. WABG's reporter asked, "What was the motive behind the murders and How strong do you believe your case against the Defendant is?" Landon responded without hesitation, the law requires proof of guilt beyond any and all reasonable doubt, and I feel certain that will be the case here". "We have very good evidence of a motive, but I think it would be imprudent to disclose that now," he further added.

With that question the press conference was ended, everyone on the steps shook hands and congratulated each other on a job well done. In their minds, they had motive, opportunity to carry out the crime and physical evidence to connect the defendant to the crimes. All the deputies, sheriff and prosecutors could almost smell the gas destined for Raymond Butler. The citizens in attendance felt as though a dark cloud had been lifted from the county and everyone left with a renewed sense of safety and great confidence in their law enforcement, much to the delight of all law enforcement and prosecution teams.

CHAPTER 20

The next day in home room at the start of school, Randy and Weasel occupied their usual place in the back of the class. Weasel asked Randy, "Did you see the news last night on channel 6?" "Hell no," replied Randy, "who watches the news?" "Well I did," Weasel answered, "Not looking good for your old man according to the cops, they say they got a strong case".

"I can't help that", replied Randy. "I gotta do what I gotta do." "I'm hoping his lawyer can get him out of it. Ain't that what lawyers do?" said Randy. "Besides, my old man has been a pain in my butt since I was born", Randy, stated as if he didn't care. "He left me and Momma to fend for ourselves, so he can fend for himself". Weasel was quick to say, "I thought your Momma was the one that left?" "Well, she was, but I think Daddy ran her off by being a jackass all the time," Randy responded. Their conversation was cut short by Ms. Ferretti at the front of the class. "Wesley, do you and Randy have something you want to share with the rest of the class?" "No ma'am," responded Weasel, "we were just talking about the news last night." That response brought "ooohs" from the rest of the class and turned Randy's face a brilliant red. "Let's stop and pay attention then", Mrs. Ferretti said. She desperately wanted to move away from the subject for poor Randy's sake. When class was over about fifteen minutes later and the students began leaving to go to History class, Mr. Ferretti cornered Randy and asked him to come back to her room right after he ate lunch and before the next class started in order to talk with her. He said he would and went on his way. When he appeared at the appointed time, she had him sit in a desk in front of hers and shut the door. "Randy, I know you are going through a hard time because of all this. Is there anything I can do to help?" she asked him. "I really wish there was," he answered. "Just something I've got to deal with, I guess". "I'd really like to help you," she added. "I'm going to get nosey and if you don't want to answer that's fine. Okay, Randy?" "Yes ma'am," he said. "Rumor has it that you will be a key witness at your father's trial". Is that true?" "It is," he answered. "That's a tough thing for anybody to do, much less a fifteen year old son, "she opined. "Would you like to tell me and the school counselor about it, "she inquired? She was curious, yes, but she felt so very sorry for him and wanted to help so bad. This is one of those duties as a teacher that no one appreciates or even considers as part of her job, but like a substitute parent to her students, she could not just turn off her emotions for these children. "I don't think so", he answered and began crying. "Can I go now?" "Sure, you can, but if you change your mind, I'm always here to talk", she told him as he gathered his books and left the room. She was about ready to cry herself because she could see the pain he was going through and wanted so badly to help him, but couldn't and it was extremely frustrating.

CHAPTER 21

Alone in the lobby of John Marshall's law office across from the courthouse, Ruby Butler was fidgety. She was there to hopefully bring her long awaited divorce from Raymond Butler, an accused multiple murder to a swift conclusion and she was hopeful he would accept the terms as set out by his mother earlier. When she was buzzed in to her attorney's main office, she quickly laid out the offer that Raymond's mother had suggested and the time frame for its acceptance. When he heard it, John Marshall thought it fair and as good or better than he could get at trial. He did wonder about the urgency in the offer's acceptance but resolved it to the fact that she didn't want Ruby backing out and that Ruby really wanted to put distance between herself and a killer. Either way, he called Jackson Jones and relayed his client's acceptance of the offer if Raymond was inclined to do likewise as his mother suggested. Jones agreed in principal, but would have to go to the jail to discuss it with Raymond before they could begin drafting the necessary paperwork. Ruby left with fingers crossed and ecstatic more so than she had been in a while. Jackson Jones had been informed that the Grand Jury had met that day and handed down capital murder indictments against his client on both counts. Landon Fall would agree to a bond hearing the next day if agreeable to counsel for the defendant. Landon had earlier in the day spoken to family members from both the Strawberry and Galtelli families and they were agreeable to nothing but would simply ask the Circuit Judge to set it with that understanding. "I can't suggest a figure, Jackson" Landon told him. "However, I will tell the judge the families will yield to his learned experience in so doing." "Putting it all on his honor, huh?" Jackson said. "That means a high bond, but probably not as much as the families want. I'm game, he added."

To know one's surprise, Raymond wouldn't consider the divorce offer without knowing what, if any bond, he might get. Evidently, freedom from jail was more important than even freedom from that bitch. However, Jackson was so confident he would accept he had his secretary begin drafting the property settlement and the decree of divorce to be used when the time came as it surely would. Like John Marshal, he wondered about the urgency of closing the deal, but never considered that she might be a witness against him in the criminal proceeding. He contacted Chancery Judge Buzzeld's office to arrange an ex parte hearing date in order to finalize the fault grounds albeit uncontested divorce. A bond hearing in front of the Circuit Judge was set for 1:00 p.m. tomorrow in Cleveland. The press was sure to show up in large numbers if they caught wind of it which would pressure Judge Baioni to set an even higher bond.

At 1:00 p.m. as scheduled, Judge Baioni took the bench in front of a packed courtroom full of lawyers, concerned citizens, families of the two victims as well as the press. Jackson Jones accused Landon and Paul of informing the press and though they would have gladly taken responsibility, the press needed no assistance in getting the word.

Mr. Jones began the proceeding by arguing that even in capital cases, defendants were entitled to some type of bond. His client was a long time resident of Bolivar County, was gainfully employed there with family also there. He could not be considered a flight risk in any manner. A reasonable bond would be $200,000 which he believed his client could make. When the district attorney's office responded through DA Landon Fall himself, he pointed out to the court that "the crimes for which the defendant was indicted involved home invasions in each instance. Two young girls had been savagely assaulted in their bedrooms while alone and strangled to death. As if that were not enough, He had raped both of them post mortem and could have been indicted for the crime of necrophilia as well. As for his connections to the county, he was presently involved in divorce proceedings so as to cut his family ties with the county. He would very soon be free to go anywhere in the world and leave Mississippi behind. His employment was speculative at best as he had been absent while held in jail and was certainly subject to firing and in the very least was not welcome back. The bottom line was he no longer had anything insuring that he would remain in Bolivar County, Mississippi. The families of the victims have assured me that they are comfortable with any bond that your honor might find appropriate under the circumstances bearing in mind the safety and well being of the community of Interstate, Mississippi and all of Bolivar County." When Landon concluded, he sat down at the counsel's table opposite Jackson Jones and both waited for the decision.

"Having heard the argument by counsel for the defendant a well as counsel for the State of Mississippi, the Court finds that a reasonable bond in the case of The State of Mississippi versus Raymond Butler, indicted on two counts of capital murder whereby the State seeks a sentence of death in the event of conviction by the jury should be no less than $750,000. Although the Court would favor no bond at all due to the heinous nature of the crimes here, if bond must be set, it should be that amount" Judge Baioni ruled. "The State is directed to prepare an order commensurate with the Court's finding herein and forward it to counsel for the defendant for agreement as to form and not content and tender to me on or before 10:00 a.m. tomorrow for entry. We all stand adjourned."

Landon and Jackson Jones were surrounded by press with mundane questions such as "Are you satisfied with the Court's ruling?" Landon responded, "We are because such a large amount is tantamount to no bond at all." He desperately wanted to add, do you think I would go on record saying his honor was just plain wrong in response to such a stupid question? Jones replied, "Of course, we are not for the same reason the DA just said. An unmakeable bond is tantamount to no bond at all."

Just before they lead Raymond away to his cell, he told Jones, "Get me the damn divorce papers, I'm getting out of something today one way or the other." Jones assured him he would and began making his way out of the courtroom.

CHAPTER 22

Randy was at home when his Grandmother Peggy called him. I'm sorry to tell you this, Randy, but the judge ruled today that they would basically be keeping your father in jail until his trial. His lawyer told me they would try to schedule the trial as quickly as possible so this whole mess will be over soon we hope. The reality was hitting Randy hard as he began crying and hung up the phone. He was really going to have to testify against his father for something he knew he didn't do, but what choice did he have now. He got on his bike, a Schwinn "stingray" with high rise handlebars and a banana seat and set out for his grandmother's house. He needed to be with somebody. The bike actually reminded him of his mom and dad in a good way. They had given it to him for Christmas two years ago. It was the finest anyone in Interstate had and he felt like he was really somebody as he rode it. In his mind he wished for those days when he got the bike, long before any of this ever happened. He shortly arrived at his grandmother's house and went inside. There was his little brother and sister he had almost forgotten about since he had been staying alone at the old homestead. His grandmother was frying chicken and making real mashed potatoes along with homemade cathead biscuits. He noticed his siblings and Grandmother had all been crying and he felt the guilt eating through his soul because he knew he was responsible. He needed to get out of there, but the lure of home cooking kept him there, at least for a short period of time. He thought about the homework he needed to do but then thought it was trivial compared to what life was throwing at him these days. Back in Cleveland, Landon, Paul and Joel were feasting on grilled cheese and ham sandwiches with a large side of fries and a cold beer at the Thicket Bar and Grill. They reveled in their victory at the bond hearing today and dreamed of the big victory they would finally get to relish once they tried Raymond on his capital murder charges. With elections coming up next year, Landon could rest easy with a conviction of Raymond Butler for two murders they had caught grief over for a year. The Thicket patrons were already quick to backslap all three of the crew there that night after the bond hearing. "What if we don't get a conviction?" Paul wondered aloud to Landon. "Did you see that crowd in the courtroom today?" Landon questioned back. "Those are the same people that will make up the jury pool. All we need to do is show our hand and they'll do the rest. No problem," he added.

Randy ate like he was starving and as soon as he finished, he headed back home on his bike. The air was a little cooler since it was September, and made him think of the months ahead and what they might bring. He was depressed and almost ill. He rode past his own home and made the short trek to Weasel's house where he found him playing in the yard with a football. They threw it back and forth a couple of times until Randy suggested they go for a ride on their bikes. They rode over to an old pond in the middle of a soybean field and saw a couple of snakes in the water. "Wish we had a gun to kill em with", said Weasel. "My old man has a.38 revolver between the mattresses on his bed, but since it's a pistol, I couldn't hit them that far out, anyway" Randy said. "I would say your dad would kill you if you messed with it, but I don't see how, now," Weasel observed. "Randy changed the subject by asking Weasel if he had told him what the pastor had told him in church. "He told me if I changed my story, my life could be in danger," Randy told Weasel. "For real, just like that", Weasel asked?"

"Exactly like that," Randy said. "I'm scared, Weasel, scared of Brother Kirksey and scared of what might happen to me and my dad, too." "I know," Weasel said. And maybe he did know to some extent, but not like Randy did. It was getting dark so the two headed back home on their bikes agreeing to talk more about the whole situation tomorrow at school. It was tough going on the dirt turn roads coming out of the field, but once they got to the main road that was blacktop it was smooth sailing. By the time Randy got back to his house, it was right at sunset and his depression was really starting to get to him. This was about the time of day that both his parents would be home and his mother would have supper ready which again reminded him of better times in the past where the amount of homework he had was his biggest concern. He left his bike in the front yard and went up on the porch and into the house and plopped down on the couch and broke down crying again. He couldn't wait for school the next day just to get around people he knew. It was then that he decided he would take Mrs. Ferretti up on her offer to talk to him in an effort t help him. How she could, he had no idea, but it had to be worth a try because continuing like this didn't seem to be an option for him with the way he was feeling now. He went to sleep that night planning on when he would get the chance to speak with her. The full moon on the Delta shone through the window like a street light. The night air was warm, but not hot as it was the month before and there was no rain in sight since the sky was cloudless.

CHAPTER 23

When the bell rang the next day at school signaling the end of home room, Randy purposely lagged behind the others in an effort to speak with Mrs. Ferretti. "Can I speak to you sometime today in private?" he asked her. "Sure", she replied. "You want me to ask the counselor as well"? "No, ma'am, just you if you don't mind". "Ok, meet me at the faculty lounge after you eat lunch and before lunch period is over," she said. "I'll be there", he said as he went out the door. At the appointed time Randy appeared outside the faculty lounge and knocked on the door. Mrs. Ferretti answered and asked him to come in and sit down. There was no one else there and she asked him to say what was on his mind. "Mrs. Ferretti, I can't handle the things I'm going through by myself anymore and I just need someone to talk to about it," he said. "Go ahead and tell me what is going on with you," she replied. "I'm sure I know some things, but" you can talk to me and it will remain between us". "This thing with my dad, he stammered. "What if I lied about it, he asked her. Thinking he surely meant if he lied to protect his dad now, she told him, "That would be perjury if it is under oath and you could be criminally charged if it was discovered and proven". "You could go to Parchman as an adult, but as a juvenile they could send you to reform school down around Jackson" possibly until you're 21 years old," she continued. "The Bible says the sins of the Father will be borne by the children for generations to come my pastor told me, I think in the book of Deuteronomy. Isn't that so," he asked. "Yes, but it also says in Ezekiel 18:20, The soul that sinneth, it shall not die. The son shall not bear the iniquity of the father, neither shall the father bear the iniquity of the son. The righteousness of the righteous shall be upon him and the wickedness of the wicked shall be upon him. "In other words, we will all be held accountable for our own sins, not that of our family," she told Randy. "But what about my sins, he asked her? Can my father not be killed for my sin, he asked his teacher"? "Not before God, but maybe by man only on this earth" was her response. Randy had begun to feel better when they first started talking about the Bible, but now he felt even worse. "I'm not sure I can go through with testifying when I know it will convict my dad and maybe even put him to death," Randy lamented. "You have to tell the truth and you can't help the outcome," she responded. "I wish I could talk to a lawyer," Randy said. "Why do you need a lawyer, Randy, you've done nothing wrong, she told him. Randy thought about that and further thought, "If she only knew." "I've got to go he said, as the bell rang signaling the end of the lunch period and the start of the new class period" "You come talk to me any time you want to, Randy, okay?" "Yes, ma'am I will," he said as he headed out the door.

Randy was a zombie the rest of the day. All he could think about was his dad going to Parchman prison to be put to death and he was responsible, then having to face God for the sins he had committed and would continue to commit. On the bus ride home with Weasel, he told him about asking Mrs. Ferretti the questions about sin and the legal questions as well. "I know you didn't tell her anything about what we, uh, me did, did you?" "Of course, not", Randy replied. "I know one thing, Weasel quickly added, you better not ever bring my name into any of this." "I never have and never would," Randy promised. "Why don't you come to my house for supper? I told Mom I was going to ask you one night this week and she's cool with it. Maybe 6:00." "I'll be there", Randy answered. Randy was glad to be going somewhere, anywhere but his house by himself. He hadn't heard from his mother in over a week.

Ruby Butler was sitting on her throne/bar stool at the bar at Oliver's bar and grill in Shaw at that precise time. She had gotten a call at work that afternoon from John Marshall that Raymond had signed the divorce papers and they were set to be presented to Judge Buzzeld to be made final at 9:00 a.m. day after tomorrow. She would need to be present with at least one witness in order to get the divorce on habitual cruel and inhuman treatment grounds. Any friend would do as long as they were familiar with Raymond's treatment of her resulting in her separation from him. No problem, she thought, she would get one of the ladies in her Sunday School class down at the church to go or draft one of the waitresses from here at Oliver's Bar. They all knew Raymond was a jackass and would gladly testify. In the end she got Gaylene Robinson from Oliver's to go, foregoing one of her Sunday School class members who might want to give her a lecture on how to live her life, post-divorce.

Ruby borrowed the phone at the bar and called Peggy Butler, her soon to be ex mother in law and shared the news of the divorce settlement. She seemed appreciative but was obviously more concerned with other matters in his life. Ruby tried very hard to hide her excitement but was certain it showed through to Peggy.

Randy got to Weasel's house right at 6:00 p.m. and almost immediately was seated at the table with Weasel's mom and Dad and Weasel, too. He looked at the three others at the table and he wanted to remind Weasel how lucky he was to be there with his parents and eating a home cooked meal of roast beef, potato salad and green beans along with homemade yeast rolls.

CHAPTER 24

At the precisely scheduled time two days later, Ruby and her witness, Gaylene Robinson appeared in the courtroom of Chancery Judge Lee Buzzeld at the courthouse in Cleveland with attorney John Marshall. John Marshall approached the bench and advised the Judge that he had a divorce wherein all the issues had been resolved except the grounds of the divorce itself and they would need to put on limited proof of grounds per Mississippi law but it should not take over ten minutes s the divorce was uncontested by the husband. His client and her witness were then sworn and began their testimony in **_Butler vs. Butler_**. Very shortly, the testimony, obviously uncontested was completed and the property settlement agreement and the proposed decree of divorce were submitted to his honor for approval and entry. With a swift stroke of a pen, Ruby was returned to the status of a single person, no longer the wife of a suspected murderer. More importantly to the State of Mississippi, she was now a competent witness against Raymond Butler in the criminal prosecution under the Mississippi Rules of Evidence. Chief Deputy James Joel was in the courtroom and observed the proceedings. He knew the importance of the divorce to the prosecution and hastily called his buddy Paul Lane to tell him the good news. The stench of gas from Parchman Farm meant for Raymond Butler was getting stronger every day. Her one and only regret was the task of telling her children that their parents were divorced, particularly Randy since he was the oldest and better able to understand the ramifications of the situation. However, she correctly assumed, Randy had more important things on his mind and though he was disappointed to hear of the finality of the divorce, it barely cracked the top ten of his worries. It did however manage to increase his depressed state by at least three fold. Paul Lane was in DA Landon Fall's office for a skull session on the upcoming scheduling of cases for trial and motion hearings. Since Raymond Butler was being held virtually without bond, it was necessary to move his case to trial as quickly as possible. That was the sentiment of Jackson Jones, defendant's attorney and Landon and Paul were in full agreement. A recent office conference with families of the Strawberry and Galtelli families reflected no interest in pursuing a plea deal with the monster who had murdered their little girls. Let him be put to death. There was always the chance that they would change their minds as the case moved along, but for now they were happy to seek the death penalty.

"I think we are looking at a Late October, early November trial date on Butler at the earliest", Landon suggested. "Fine with me, but let's look at the home football games Ole Miss has during that period of time, no use getting bogged down with work and screw up our weekends when we could do it another time," Landon said. "I'm looking at the schedule now and it looks like the Rebels play Georgia in Athens on October 10, Southern Miss in Oxford on October 17, and the next home game in Oxford after that is Homecoming on November 7 against Houston. I'm good with any week except the week following homecoming, November 7", other than that, any time in October will be good with me," Paul replied. Across the nation, but particularly in the South, College football dominated fall talk, rivaled only by hunting seasons. In Mississippi it was as close to a religion as anything could be. Games dictated wedding dates, preempted all other social events and caused separations and family squabbles when rival teams played. Evidently, it also affected murder trial scheduling.

Randy Butler got up from his desk in the back of the room in geography class and walked toward the door. He had his coat over his head to hide his face. "Are you going somewhere, Randy", Mrs. Ferretti asked? "I'm getting out of here", was Randy's reply. She wasn't sure what the problem was and his reply would have ordinarily drawn her wrath, but under the circumstances she let it slide and just said, "you call me if you need me." The entire class was in shock but not a word was spoken. Nobody talked although everybody wondered what was going on. A few seconds later the entire class heard Randy heaving as he threw up in the hallway. Mrs. Ferretti rushed out into the hall and got a chair for Randy to sit in and asked the teacher next door to get a janitor to come up and clean up the mess. "I'm fine," Randy volunteered, "I just need to get some air and get away for a while." "What brought it on," his teacher asked. "All this stuff with my dad," he responded. "I'm so sorry, Randy and I wish there was something I could do," she said. "I do, too," said Randy. "But there ain't. I got myself into this, I'll get myself out some way", Randy replied. She told him to go sit on the steps of the school outside and get some air and if he felt sick again or needed her to please come and get her. "If any other teacher asks you what you are doing there, tell her I sent you out there and she should talk to me. I'll come check on you at the end of this class," she instructed. He did as he was told and stayed until she retrieved him as promised. "I'm better now", he said." "How would you like to come home and stay with me tonight," she asked? "No ma'am, but thanks," he said to her. "I just want things to get back to normal". Mrs. Ferretti almost cried at that. I'm afraid things will never be back to normal for you, Randy, she thought, but dared not say.

On the bus ride home, Randy tried to explain to Weasel how stressed he was, but although he appeared to understand, Randy knew there was no way he could really comprehend. When the bus stopped at his house, they saw Randy's Mom's car in the drive and both wondered what good tidings she was bringing to Randy today. "You come to my house if you need too, buddy", Weasel suggested. "I will," Randy replied. He got off the bus and walked slowly to the door of his house where he knew his mother was waiting inside.

"There's my man of the house," his mom almost yelled as he walked in. She had a bottle of cheap champagne that she was drinking directly from the bottle and apparently had been drinking for some time as it was only half full. "You drinking, Mom?" he asked. "I am indeed", she exclaimed. "I'm celebrating my divorce from that bastard dad of yours. Got it today."

Randy didn't know what to say so he ran to his bedroom and slammed the door shut. He piled up in the middle of his bed and buried his face in the pillow. How could she be so cruel and thoughtless he wondered? She knocked on his door but he wouldn't answer. "What's the matter Randy, you knew we were getting a divorce," she said. "Just go away," he told her and she did just that without saying a word. Got into her car, peeled out of the drive and didn't stop until she got to Oliver's in Shaw.

Randy quit crying eventually and sat up in his bed. He looked around at the pictures and posters on the wall of his room from better days in the past. There was a picture of him and Weasel hanging above his dresser where they had shot a couple of squirrels a few years back. A poster of Elvis Presley, a hero to all in the South. This room used to be his place of solace, but not anymore. Now it reminded him of a place and good time he knew he would never enjoy again.

Eventually, Randy got up and sat at the desk in his room that he used for studying in the past, but that seemed like such a long time ago to him now. He retrieved a pen and spiral bound composition tablet from the middle drawer. He had been thinking about something for a while now and this latest development convinced him that this was the thing to do. He tore a couple of sheets from the tablet and begin to write the following:

I am so depressed now that I believe this is the only way for relief from it. I have managed to screw up not only my life, but the lives of both my parents now causing them to divorce and leave me and my brother and sister alone. I know I am worthless because my dad and mom have both told me. Maybe now everyone will be better. I am sorry and I hope everybody forgives me. This is nobody's fault but mine. Tell Weasel and Mrs. Ferretti I said goodbye. Randy Butler. September 29,1970.

The entire message had been printed by his hand, but he signed his name in cursive and printed the date under it. He put it on the front door and closed the screen door. Then he went to his parent's bedroom, retrieved his dad's.38 caliber revolver from between the mattresses, went back to his bedroom, and once again laid on his bed with his head on the pillow. He checked the cylinder to make sure the pistol was loaded, cocked the hammer, placed the barrel against the temple of his head and pulled the trigger.

Randy never even heard the shot or felt the fire from the end of the barrel. He was dead instantly after pulling the trigger. He actually never knew when the trigger was pulled. He no longer had to worry about testifying at his dad's trial. He no longer bore the guilt of his sin and the disastrous consequences his lie had for everyone, including him. His bed and mattress together with all the linens was ruined from the blood and the brain matter, but that was somebody else's problem, not his. It was a harsh end to a harsh life he had lived. Some of his life had been harsh at Randy's own hand, and some had been harsh because of other people. Maybe it was fitting that no one else played a part in how he died except Randy himself. It's sad that few people understand youth depression. The burdens they bear are every bit as heavy as those of adults, at least in their own minds. In the end, few of those who choose to die by their own hand understand that suicide is more often than not a permanent solution to a temporary problem. In the end however, they all weigh the consequences of dying as opposed to that of continuing to live and choose death. Randy did just that and saw where death was more welcoming than the life he had or would have in the future. He could be blamed for making his bed and then having to lie in it and it is what it is, but you couldn't help but mourn for someone who knew he was worthless because many had told him and few told him otherwise.

CHAPTER 25

The next day at school when Mrs. Ferretti called the roll in home room class and Randy didn't answer, she feared the worst but like everyone, never saw the worst coming as it had. She merely thought he was ill and unable to come to school. She wondered who to call to check on him, but was puzzled. She had no number for his mother and his father was certainly no option. The only person she knew to contact was Peggy Butler his grandmother who lived down the road from him. She called, but Peggy knew nothing but promised to go check. She drove the short half mile to his house and parked in the drive. As she walked up onto the dilapidated porch, she saw Randy's letter sticking out of the screen door. She sat down in a chair on the porch and started to read. She broke down a few lines into it. When she finished it, she had the intelligence to leave without going inside although she did call for him at the door with no response. She got back in her car and went home and immediately called the Bolivar County Sheriff's office. She was transferred to Chief Deputy Joel and told him her grandson was missing and may have committed suicide. She explained the letter she found and all that had transpired that morning. He immediately dispatched an ambulance and a sheriff's unit to the home and then left himself enroute to there as well. She promised she would meet him there and make sure no one went into the house until he arrived. As soon as Joel was in his car, he radioed dispatch to contact Paul Lane to meet him there as well. Paul was on his way in minutes. Since lawyers rarely think of anyone else first but themselves, Paul was already conjuring the scenarios in his mind that would evolve if Randy Butler was dead, and there was no escaping the obvious: Without Randy Butler's testimony to connect the rings from the two murder victims taken at the scene of the murders to Raymond, there was no murder case against him. It was as simple as that. God, please say it isn't so, thought Paul. Then he felt guilty about putting the merits of his case ahead of the tragedy of a fifteen year old who was depressed to the point of taking his own life. It seemed as if he would never get to Interstate Woods and the drive reminded him of the first call he had made to there when he went to investigate the apparent murder/rape of Linda Strawberry over a year ago. God, when would this case ever be over, he wondered aloud. No time soon, he thought, not without that fifteen year old kid.

CHAPTER 26

Paul Lane got to the Butler residence on Trunkline Road to find two deputy units there, both with blue lights flashing. An ambulance with its own lights flashing and Peggy Butler there as promised. Joel informed him that he had stuck his head in the door and called for the boy, but had not entered the home. He and Paul then went in together and went straight to the bedroom area of the house where they found the horrible scene with Randy lying on his bed with blood everywhere. "Keep Peggy Butler out", Paul yelled to those deputies outside. Smartly, there was nothing to be accomplished by allowing the decedent's grandmother to witness the carnage, not even for identification purposes as both Joel and Paul were able to do so from past meetings with him. Paul produced his camera and began to take multiple pictures of the scene, including the apparent suicide note he was handed and read. Joel then summoned the ambulance crew to come in to retrieve the body. The coroner had been summoned but had not arrived, but Paul was comfortable with the evidence he saw at the scene together with a suicide note identified by Peggy Butler as being in Randy's own handwriting, to conclude the child had taken his own life and foul play was not involved. Once the body left by transport to the morgue at East Bolivar County hospital, the law enforcement personnel began to wrap up and leave themselves, but not until they offered to accompany Peggy back to her house, an offer she declined. Paul told Joel he would talk to him back in Cleveland, but first wanted to talk to his boss, DA Landon Fall. He got to Landon's office to find him there waiting for him, having heard to news from the sheriff's office himself. "It's tragic, Landon," Paul said as he entered the room. "A fifteen year old boy committing suicide is unthinkable. On the other hand, how does it affect our case against Raymond,' Paul asked"? "*What* case, now", Landon responded. "It's real simple. Without Randy to connect the rings taken from each murder to his father, we have zero evidence to link Raymond to their deaths. All we have left is testimony that Raymond is a kinky bastard with his wife. Makes for good daytime television, but worthless now in the courtroom in a murder trial." "Any idea why he did it, "asked Landon afterwards. "Note just said he was depressed and felt worthless, I'm sure just the totality of the circumstances he found himself in", Paul answered. Paul didn't want to say it and certainly didn't have to as far as Landon was concerned, but they would have to dismiss the indictment and set Raymond free, possibly to murder again for all they knew.

"While I'm thinking about it, chimed Landon, my Secretary said you had a call from Taylor Buttrell over in Indianola wanting to talk to you". "Crap, Paul said, I know he wants to talk about the murder of the young girl over there a few weeks ago that had similarities to the Interstate murders. I had told him we had this one wrapped and might wrap up his case, too if they were the same killer. Guess it doesn't matter now." "Anything to connect Raymond to that case," Landon asked? "Nothing but wishful thinking, especially now," Paul retorted. "You call Jackson Jones and tell him the good news for Raymond and I'll see when we can get before Judge Baioni to ask for the dismissal", Landon said in disgust. Paul nodded in agreement and left the office and went straight to the sheriff's office to see Chief Deputy Joel. He hated to admit defeat, particularly in this case, but the sooner he did, the better he thought. In Joel' s office he repeated to him the conversation he and

Landon had just had as it pertained to the Interstate murders. He was no happier with the case assessment by Paul and Landon than they were, but there was no getting around the fact that without Randy Butler, Raymond Butler was off the hook on his two count indictment for murder. All were seasoned in prosecution and though it was distasteful, that fact was inescapable. "At least I don't have to tell Jones's silly ass that he is the winner here, "crowed Joel. "No, that displeasure falls to me, and I'll call him when I get back to my office". However, upon returning to his office, Paul returned the call to Taylor Buttrell over in Indianola first. Once he got him on the phone, he began to explain the evidence they had against Raymond Butler and was optimistic that if he was convicted in Bolivar County and sent to prison, because of the similarities in the Garrett murder in Sunflower County to the Interstate murders, if they were committed by the same perpetrator, his county could rest at ease because the murderer was off the street. Then he had to tell him that Paul's star witness was dead by his own hand and his case had crumbled overnight. Accordingly, if Raymond was in fact the same killer in Bolivar and Sunflower Counties, he was about to be put back on the street, maybe to kill again, possibly in both counties. To say Taylor was disappointed was a true understatement, but no more than Paul was.

"I guess I better get my Garrett file back out and get to work, I thought maybe I was through with it, but here we go again, Taylor told him. All I've got so far are crime scene photos of a dead girl, some footprints and tire tracks," Taylor confessed. "You don't happen to know Raymond's shoe size, do you?" Paul replied, "probably at least a twelve and he always wears safety boots, the steel toe type required by his employer." Negative, replied Taylor, photos reflect a nine or 10 and definitely a shoe. What vehicle did Raymond drive," he further asked? "A Ford pickup in four wheel drive", answered Paul. "Strike two" said Taylor. "Tracks left at the scene I photographed appeared to be left by a small vehicle with narrow tires like a Datsun or a Volkswagen. No mud grips". "Oh, well, we'll both keep on looking", Paul observed. "Call me if you need me, Buddy and I'll do the same". They both hung up and wondered when they would talk again with some new leads. It had been over a year since the Bolivar County, Interstate murders, and Paul was now back to square one, when only yesterday he was talking about trial dates. It could not be more frustrating.

CHAPTER 27

News of the tragic death of Randy Butler spread through Interstate and Shaw like the flu. At the Sandpit Store, the patrons lamented that they knew the boy was having a hard time especially in school between the arrest of his father and the separation of his parents because their own children had told them, but no one had seen this coming. At the Trunkline Gas Company during breaks and at lunch, the fellow employees of Raymond Butler, even those who disliked him expressed sympathy for him for his troubles over the last few weeks. He had basically lost his job because the company had said they didn't want him back due to the time his criminal charges were taking. He and his wife were separated and now divorced. He was broke because he had liquidated his retirement and spent it on lawyer fees and his ex-wife. Most even wondered how he could pay to bury his son. His friends at work and even at the Interstate Baptist Church had shunned him and wanted nothing to do with him. He had been publicly humiliated on local television and in the papers, locked away because his own son had fingered him as a killer and now his son had taken his life. Even if he was acquitted, most wondered what kind of life he had to come back to at this point. Some of the fellas proclaimed out loud that the premise of innocent until proven guilty was bullshit and always had been. However, every soul in the breakroom thought Raymond was guilty as hell, based on what they had heard and seen on television and in the papers.

With the possible exception of Mrs. Ferretti, no one was crushed by the death of young Randy Butler anymore than Wesley Bowman, a/k/a Weasel, best friend to Randy. He had seen the blue lights and the police cars and ambulance at Randy's house when he got home from school. He knew Randy had missed school that day and asked his Mom what was going on. She told him with little fanfare that Randy had shot himself the night before and was dead. Weasel first wondered if there might be foul play, remembering what Randy had told him what the pastor had said. When he heard about the suicide note, he knew Randy just couldn't take it anymore. He then became angry that Randy had not at least talked to him about it before he did it so that he might help him, but he knew there was nothing he could have done to help him.

Weasel remembered that the last thing he had said to Randy was to come to his house if he needed to talk. He then retreated to his room and locked the door, foregoing supper and didn't come out until the next morning when he announced he couldn't take school that day. When his mother agreed for him to stay home, he went back to his room for the remainder of the day, coming out only for supper that night.

In the teacher's lounge at Shaw High School the day after Randy's death, Mrs. Ferretti was virtually inconsolable. She had learned of Randy's death the previous day when a fellow teacher had called her at home with the news. That teacher apparently had a family member working at the Sheriff's office and learned from him. She and Mrs. Ferretti had talked about Randy before and she knew of Mrs. Ferretti's fondness and concern for him. Mrs. Sandroni, the girl's PE teacher took Mrs. Ferretti's homeroom class and allowed her to remain in the lounge and not face that memory today. After that class Mrs. Ferretti kept the remaining class schedule she had and was better as the day went, although many things reminded her of her student friend who she had tried unsuccessfully to help. Teachers are often warned not to get too involved in the lives of their students, but human nature usually dictates otherwise. She had assumed, correctly so, that she was the only positive influence on Randy Butler in the final days of his short life.

When Weasel got up for school the following day, he was even more angry about the death of his best friend. Angry to the point that he wanted to make someone pay. Not Randy's father, for Weasel knew he was innocent, maybe not Randy's mother because Weasel didn't know about the callous way she had delivered the news of the divorce to Randy, but perhaps the pastor who had threatened poor Randy, sending him over the edge. Somebody would pay, he swore to himself, but just how, he was unsure. His mind was reeling with the thought of Randy's funeral service coming up very soon at the Interstate Baptist Church, a service he dreaded, but wouldn't think about missing because of his friend, Randy, that he already missed more than he could believe. He had seen the huge gathering of cars and trucks parked in the drive and yard of Peggy Butler, signifying a southern custom of family and friends visiting the decedent's family following the death of a loved one while bringing food for the mourning family. Ordinarily, people would come to the decedent's residence, but poor Randy really didn't have one because of the separation of his parents and the other circumstances arising over the last couple of months that had caused the absence of his father, so they piled into his Grandmother's home just down the road. Also, it was customary in those times in Mississippi and throughout the south to bring the body back to the home prior to the funeral after preparation at the funeral home for lying in state in the casket for viewing by friends and family for a couple of days. Randy's Grandmother had declined to do this in Randy's case because she wanted a closed casket service, supposedly because of the damage inflicted on Randy's face and head by the bullet he fired to end his misery and life.

Channel 6 news at 5:00 p.m. reported that Raymond Butler was scheduled the day after tomorrow to appear before Circuit Judge John Baioni for a hearing requested by the district attorney's office. Investigator Paul Lane of the DA's office, in charge of the investigation had no comment but invited the public to tune in the day after tomorrow at 9:00 a.m. for breaking news. Weasel assumed it was to advise every one of the death of Randy. But it also told him who he might want to talk to about Randy. He made a vow to contact Paul Lane with the DA's office in Cleveland some way tomorrow after the funeral which was scheduled for 10:00 a.m.

CHAPTER 28

During the night, Weasel dreamed of his dead friend. He dreamed he had ridden on his bike to Randy's house to find him there watching *Hogan's Heroes* on television. They talked and Weasel told him of his plan to contact Paul Lane and tell him what he knew about the rings and the pastor. Randy warned him not to get in too deep like he had done. He then wondered aloud to Weasel with a mischievous smile, "whose life is in danger now"? Weasel assured him he would be careful and tell nothing but the truth regardless of the consequences. "Please do", responded Randy and with that he left Randy's house on his bike and returned home. The next thing he remembered was waking up in his bed. He knew his conversation with Randy had been nothing but a dream, but he felt better about the whole situation afterwards.

Later in the morning, shortly after both his parents had headed off to work and the school bus had made its stop without Weasel getting on as he had been given permission to miss school that day due to the death of his friend, he immediately began looking through the Cleveland phone directory, searching for the number of the district attorney's office. When he found it, he jotted it down so he could call it a little later that day. About 8:30 that morning, he made the call and when someone answered, he asked to speak to Mr. Lane and the secretary gave him the number to Paul's office over on the other side of the courthouse square. Weasel wrote it down and immediately called it, telling the receptionist he needed to talk to Mr. Lane about an emergency. When his voice came on the phone, Weasel began to tell his story. "Mr. Lane, my name is Wesley Bowman and I need to talk to you about some things I know about the murders in Interstate a year ago. Randy Butler's father is innocent and I know the truth about the rings", Weasel began. The mention of the rings by someone other than the prosecution team was enough to catch Paul's attention since only law enforcement investigating the case knew that fact. "How old are you, son and where can I meet with you.?" Paul asked. "I'll be happy to come to your house and talk to you and your parents". This caught Weasel off guard because he hadn't planned on involving either of his parents, so he told Paul. "I'm fifteen years old and I don't need my parents knowing this information", Weasel stated. Paul was forced to make a quick decision to tell the caller he had to have his parents present or talk to the lad without them and take a chance that the boy's statement, whatever it might be, could not be used against him if he confessed to a crime without his parent or parents being present. He immediately decided to roll the dice and talk to this kid without his parents. If he appeared to be incriminating himself, he could always stop the questioning and get the parents before proceeding any further, and then hope his statement afterward could be used if necessary. "Damn juveniles, Paul said to himself. "They are such a pain in the ass to deal with". "Ok son, we will play by your rules for now. Where do you live so I can come out there this afternoon and talk to you", Paul asked? "945 Trunkline Road, in the Interstate community, Weasel told him, Weasel replied. "Okay, I'll be there about 1:00 this afternoon", Paul said and hung up the phone. Weasel immediately began getting dressed to attend his friend's funeral at the church just down the road. As soon as he hung up the phone, it occurred to Paul that he had neglected to get the boy's phone number. However, he had his name and address and that was enough to find him. He headed out of the office to grab lunch at Rudolph's BBQ House out on 61 Highway before he made the now familiar trek to Interstate to see what young Wesley Bowman had to say. He thought about calling Joel and asking him if he wanted to go, but decided against it since two adults might intimidate the boy too much and he could handle it himself. After feasting on the lunch buffet consisting of pork BBQ, creamed potatoes, other veggies and homemade rolls, and washing it down with sweet tea, Paul made a bathroom run, paid his bill and then headed out to talk with Wesley. He was extremely curious to say the least and although he was thinking about this kid, Wesley, he couldn't shake the thoughts of young. Randy Butler. He gave a quick thought of attending the funeral, but decided his presence there may be unwanted. About twenty minutes later, he arrived at a white clapboard house with large oak and pecan trees in the yard, under which sat an assortment of farm implements and an old John Deere 4020 tractor. The mailbox had 945 painted in red on the side. He turned into the drive and saw a young boy with sandy hair cut very short in a shirt and tie, still fresh from the funeral, come out of the house and run toward his car. It was 1:05 p.m. according to the clock on the dash of his car. He told Wesley to get in the front seat and he obeyed. "How are you, Wesley?" Paul asked him. "Call me Weasel," he retorted. "That's what friends call me, so if you are my friend, call me that". "Okay, Weasel, you called me, so what's up?", Paul said. "What do you know?" "I know everything," Weasel responded. "How about we take this conversation to my office in Cleveland? I'll bring you back as soon as we are through", Paul suggested. Weasel really had no problem in going to Paul's office to talk, but was just a tad distrustful of "the law" since he had never dealt with an officer, but had heard numerous nightmare stories about them. "You are gonna record me, aren't you? Weasel inquired. "What makes you think so?" Paul returned. "Randy Butler said he was recorded", Weasel responded. "So, you and Randy were good friends?" "The best", Weasel told him. "I'm sorry about him, Paul said as he sped up on his way back to Cleveland. Weasel didn't say much until they got to Paul's office after that. He just looked out the window at the never ending rows of cotton and soybeans along

Highway 61 as they traveled north back to Cleveland. When they pulled up in front of Paul's office, they both got out and went inside. Upon entering Paul's office, Paul immediately began setting up the reel to reel tape recorder on his desk and threading the tape for recording. "I knew it", exclaimed Weasel! "Just like Randy said". Paul's secretary who happened to be a notary, came in and swore the young man in. "Not afraid of being recorded are you, Weasel?", Paul asked him. "No, sir, just makes it all seem so serious and formal", Weasel answered. "It is," chimed Paul, "so tell me the truth and nothing but the truth."

"No problem," Weasel told him. Paul dictated the time, date and who was present in the room and that Weasel had requested to talk to him about the Raymond Butler case and further advised if Weasel disagreed with anything Paul put into the recording, he was to correct him accordingly. Weasel acknowledged and the interview began.

CHAPTER 29

"Tell me what you wanted to talk to me about, Wesley. Weasel started and barely drew a breath for the next twenty or thirty minutes.

"One day after school, me and Randy rode our bikes to the Interstate Baptist Church because that was the closest place that we could get a coca cola and it was so hot. His dad had made him stay outside because he was trying to sleep. We had some change but when we got to the church, they had raised the price on the cokes so we were short. Randy suggested looking around for some loose change in the church. We looked in the pews of the sanctuary, the Sunday school classrooms but came up empty. We found the pastor's study was unlocked so Randy went in and looked in the preacher's desk.

Pastor didn't have any change there, but Randy found a plastic sandwich bag with two rings in it and he kept them. He said he was going to sell them at a pawn shop in Cleveland because they looked like they were expensive. He asked me if I wanted in on it and I told him no way, those rings were poison and no good could come from them. Besides, I knew God would really get me if I stole from the church like that. Randy put em in his pants pocket and we hightailed it out of there after getting a drink of water in the boys' restroom. He told me later that his mom took him to the pawnshop a few days later and he sold them for forty five bucks for both rings.

He had to sign a statement under oath that he got them from his dad's nightstand, which was a lie, but he didn't want to admit he took them from the church. Then you guys got involved and he had to give another statement under oath to the law that he got them from his dad's nightstand because he couldn't change his story and tell the truth then because that would be perjury and he could go to jail or reform school.

The next thing we know, his Dad is arrested for murder because the rings were taken from those murders in Interstate over a year ago. So, Randy is stuck and not able to tell the truth to save his old man without going to jail himself for at least perjury and was also afraid you guys might even charge him with murder. Then a little over a week ago, the pastor calls him in to his office and tells Randy he better stick to his story because if he didn't, Randy's life might be in danger. Then he finds his parents got their divorce and all that was weighing heavy on Randy and he couldn't take it anymore, so he killed himself a couple days ago.

At that point, Weasel stopped and took a long breath and asked Paul for a coke, which he got and then sat quietly waiting on Paul to say something.

"What is this pastor's name," Paul asked? "It's Brother W.D. Kirksey, replied Weasel. Paul had to fight the urge to leave the room and immediately get a warrant for the arrest of the pastor, but he waited. He just sat there in silence with Weasel and marveled at the story this kid had just told him. He had no doubt the boy was not making it up, because he knew particulars about the rings that only Randy would know, even the correct sales price. Better yet, the story made too much sense to be fabricated by a fifteen year old. From the finding of the rings, to the sales price, to the reason for lying first and then sticking to the story, to the reason a fifteen year old takes his own life, it all made perfect sense and not many accomplished fiction writers could make it up, much less a fifteen year old kid. Paul asked a follow up question after a bit. "Weasel, you know what happened to Randy and what he went through. You do not want to make the same mistake do you, he asked? "oh, no, sir," was Weasel's instant response. "Everything I just told you is the God's honest truth". About that time, Linda, Paul's secretary stuck her head in the door and advised Paul that Landon Fall was on the phone for him. Paul answered and Landon informed him that he and Jackson Jones had talked with Judge Baoini and had a hearing for dismissal at 9:00 a.m. tomorrow. Paul acknowledge and said he needed to talk further with Landon later this afternoon. They agreed to meet at 5:00 at Landon's office about an hour and a half from then. Paul hung up and jotted a reminder on his notepad to call Taylor Buttrell about Weasel's statement and have him check on the pastor's dealings and connections in Sunflower County which might implicate him in the Garrett murder that Taylor had. With that, Paul ended the recording, thanked Weasel and then instructed him not to talk with anyone else about the case. Afterwards, they left the office, returned to Paul's car and Weasel was transported back home to Interstate. He was quiet the entire ride home, reflecting on the earlier morning when he had attended Randy's funeral. The church had been packed as churches usually are in the case of a young person's death. He had to sit toward the front instead of his customary back row as all Baptists attempted to do. That was fine with Weasel because it put him closer to the casket bearing Randy, his friend which would be the closest he would be to him ever again. He was alone, but he noticed a number of classmates with their parents that had come to the service, most notably, Olivia Powell, the girl of Randy's dreams, though unbeknownst to her because Randy was far too shy to talk to her. Weasel thought about how proud Randy would be to know Olivia was there and how impressed he would be to see so many of his classmates there, most of which never gave Randy the time of day before his death. Ms. Ferretti, Mrs. Sandroni and Principal Hill were also there. Randy would indeed be impressed.

Shortly after everyone entered the church along with the silver metal casket, Brother Kirksey got up to speak. He reminded everyone in attendance that Randy was not dead, but had just moved on to Heaven because God wanted him there. He talked about how brave Randy was in life and how he had suffered emotionally over the past couple of months, but was now at peace. He told the crowd how he had talked with Randy just a week or so in his office and how courageous he had been about testifying in court in the next few weeks or so.

It was at this point that Weasel had to put all his energy into restraining himself from jumping up and announcing to everyone that the preacher was the real killer and had threatened Randy not to tell the real truth which helped put Randy over the edge and made him kill himself. He managed to restrain himself and instead just sat quietly seething with anger at the hypocrite in the pulpit. He again swore vengeance for Randy and couldn't wait until the afternoon to hang the preacher out to dry for good. He sobbed silently for his dead friend and prayed for Randy and his family throughout the rest of the service, even asking God to help him destroy the preacher.

CHAPTER 30

On his way back to Cleveland after taking Weasel home, Paul reflected on the Butler murder prosecution which made him sick to his stomach. When the Interstate murders occurred, Paul had been so cautious in refraining from jumping to conclusions when it came to the guilt of Tyrone Braid and he had been correct in so doing. However, when it came to Raymond Butler, he never hesitated. Not only did he go at him with fangs bared, but had made the often made mistake of trying the case in the court of public opinion for the sake of job security for public appeal. He reflected on the big show they manufactured with the press when they arrested Raymond. Now they had a man who they had financially broken, without a doubt cost him his job, and besmirched his reputation all across the county and state to the point he was an outcast in his own community and he had been innocent from the beginning and was now about to be set free. It would be easy to blame his son, but looking back, their case was full of holes from the beginning, otherwise it would not have fallen apart so easily. He made a solemn vow to himself that he would certainly go after the preacher, but in fairness, would hold his cards and play them only at trial. Then he thought, the public is not going to believe him or the press at this point anyway after they appeared so sure they had their man with Raymond. He only hoped he had not tainted the jury pool so that if they did have the evidence to find the pastor guilty, they would convict him as opposed to having doubts because of Raymond's prosecution earlier.

When he got to Landon's office, he first told him of the revelations as told by Weasel. Then he lamented what they had done to Raymond, an obvious innocent man, to the point that he mentioned possibly resigning as a prosecutor. Maybe he didn't have the stomach for it anymore. Landon brushed it off and told him to take a deep breath. Sure, they could have handled it differently, but the evidence they had certainly indicated guilt, but maybe they should proceed with caution with the pastor and not show their hand as quickly. Paul agreed and the two left to go home knowing they would meet again in the courtroom in the morning at nine with Jackson Jones to ask that Raymond's charges be dismissed. Paul grabbed a coke from Landon's refrigerator and began to drink it as he headed out the door. If it was just a little later in the day, Paul would have preferred a strong drink of Jack Daniels, but the coke alone would do for now.

Paul went back to his office before heading home to try and call Taylor Buttrell over at the Sunflower County sheriff's office. When he got him on the phone, he couldn't wait to tell him about Weasel's implications of the pastor and ask him to check on his connections to the Roundaway community in Sunflower county or better yet, to the Garrett victim directly. He agreed and they ended the call with mutual promises to talk again before the week's end.

CHAPTER 31

At exactly nine a.m. the next morning Judge Baioni took the bench and called up The State of Mississippi vs. Raymond Butler. Landon Fall stepped forward from counsel table and stated for the record, "Your Honor, on behalf of the State of Mississippi, we would like to request that all indictments against the defendant Raymond Butler be dismissed with prejudice. Upon the death of Randy Butler, son of the defendant, we find that he was an extremely crucial witness and without his testimony we are unable to say to the Court in good faith that we can present adequate and sufficient evidence to prove guilt beyond any reasonable doubt. Accordingly, in the interest of justice and judicial economy, we must ask that the indictments be dismissed and the defendant be allowed to go free on this day. The air was simultaneously drawn out of the courtroom as the crowd in attendance drew in their breath. The families of the victims were obviously disappointed but they had been briefed by Landon and Paul before the hearing as to what to expect so they were fine in the end. With a rap of his gavel, the judge granted the motion and ordered the bailiff to escort the defendant back to the sheriff's office to pick up his belongings and then to release him forthwith. Landon and Paul stopped to explain the reason for their requested dismissal to the press as they made their way to their respective offices.

Upon arrival at his office, Paul was so disgusted with his inability to solve the Interstate Woods murder case that he decided to drive back out to Interstate to have a look around and perhaps have a chat with the pastor whose name had risen to the top of any suspect list he might have in connection with the murders provided he could do so without spooking the man or tipping him off to his suspicions. As he passed Randy Butler's home and the home of his friend, Weasel, he couldn't help but feel sympathy for the two for having to deal with the hand that fate had dealt them in this matter. Shortly thereafter he pulled into the parking lot of the Interstate Baptist Church where only a single vehicle was parked, a light blue 1968 Volkswagen Beetle parked in the space reserved for the Pastor. The thought came to him from out of the blue but hit Paul like a ton of bricks as he remembered Taylor Buttrell saying that the tire tracks photographed at the scene of the Garrett murder obviously belonged to a small car such as a Datsun or a Volkswagen. Paul parked next to it and attempted to go inside the church. As usual, the church was open and he began to look around for the pastor. He found him in his study behind his desk reading. He arose as Paul came in and introduced himself to Paul. As he stood there shaking his hand, Paul quickly noted that he wore dress shoes of course and would estimate they were size ten at the most, maybe even an eight and a half or nine. Paul started to engage him in idle conversation, but thought better of it and excused himself to leave. As he got back into his car, he noticed the tires of the Volkswagen were size 165SR-15 and had very good tread as if they were fairly new or very recently replaced. They were in fact, noticeably narrow compared to other cars on the road today. He climbed into his own car, started it up and headed down Interstate Road on his way back to Cleveland. He called Taylor Buttrell when he got back and set up a meeting with him in Indianola the next day. He held off telling Taylor about the pastor's car until then but it was difficult because any potential lead for either of them was big news in light of the implosion of the Butler case.

The next morning, Paul took pastries from Delta Cream Doughnuts to Landon's office and told him he would be out that morning because he was going to Indianola to meet with Buttrell on the Garrett murder in the Roundaway community of Sunflower County. "Oh?", said Landon, his boss. "I didn't realize the legislature had added Sunflower County to our 11th Circuit District, Landon added with a smile. "Paul quickly said, "It's just that our Interstate murders and the Roundaway murder seems so closely connected that it benefits us to compare notes." Landon replied, "I totally understand. Just messing with you. Go ahead and do what you need to do." Paul inhaled the last of the cinnamon roll he had started and looked for a napkin to wipe his mouth. "Thanks, boss. Call me if you need me. With that, he left and headed to the next county, anxious to compare notes with Taylor, who at that very moment was meeting with Sammy and Wilma Garrett, the parents of Jennifer Garrett, at their request to update them on any movement or revelations concerning the investigation into the murder of their daughter. As you might expect, both parents were frustrated with the lack of an arrest or even very much evidence to implicate a suspect. He advised them that his hopes that Raymond Butler might prove to be guilty of the murder of their daughter because of the similarities to the *Interstate murders had been dashed when his indictments had been dismissed that morning because of lack of evidence. Both parents fumed and ranted about the crime, but understood Taylor's lack of success was not the result of lack of effort. Like most parents in such a situation, they expressed their hatred for the killer and hoped God would strike him down, whoever the killer was. They left Taylor's office with his assurance that he would notify them should anything new develop in the investigation of this case. The parents of Jennifer Garrett were salt of the earth people, hard-working middle-middle class people who had enjoyed a good law abiding life until some monster roaming the backroads of Sunflower County, Mississippi decided to crush their world by murdering their daughter. They were God-fearing people who were unaccustomed to this type of tragedy. Sammy farmed a small plot of inherited land and Wilma had always stayed at home and raised Jennifer until her death and had only recently taken a job with the US Post Office in nearby Doddsville. Both were unable to talk about their daughter without breaking down sobbing. They knew it would get better with time, but in the meantime, the memories made it hard to move on with their lives.*

Taylor had intentionally failed to mention any possibility about WD Kirksey being a suspect as there was just not enough evidence to tie him to the Garrett murder and he didn't want them to get their hopes up, only to be let down if the evidence linking him to Jennifer's murder never materialized.

CHAPTER 32

When Paul got to the Sunflower County sheriff's office in Indianola which took more time than he expected because he got behind several tractors and cotton pickers on the two lane rural roads which always slows a driver down due to the inability to pass on those winding Delta Roads. Nonetheless, Taylor ushered him into his office where he already had his files out to discuss with Paul.

"Before we get started, let me tell you this," Paul suggested. "I had an opportunity yesterday to meet the Pastor, Brother Kirksey in his office at the Interstate Baptist Church. I dropped by just to eyeball him, not to question him and I found something interesting." "Seems like the reverend drives a 1968 Volkswagen Beetle with 165SR-15 tires, very narrow with like new tread. I'd love to compare them to the photos of tire tracks at the scene of the murder," he continued. Physically, he's 6'2", maybe, probably 55-60 years old. Shoe size is also small for his physical size, maybe 8 ½ to 10, maximum. He's large enough to commit the murders on small young girls for sure.

"Here is something I found", Taylor interjected. "Jennifer Garrett just this past summer attended a revival over at the Interstate Baptist Church in July and sang a solo one night, so the good reverend can't say he never knew her. That comes from her parents in Roundaway. She was so cute she would have stood out to anyone, but especially when she was showcased like that." "Do we have enough evidence with this Weasel kid's testimony to get a search warrant for the preacher's car and office, maybe his home?" Taylor asked. "Maybe in Bolivar County, yes, but we are still too weak to get one from Sunflower, I think," Paul answered. I agree, said Taylor, but it doesn't matter from which case we get it, any evidence can be used in either one, right? "Absolutely," Paul agreed. "I think my Circuit Judge will give us one for all three with Weasel's testimony." "Let's go after it then, chimed in Taylor. One caveat, though, we don't need to make a big splash in doing this after the Raymond Butler debacle. The preacher is popular I'm sure, as most Baptist preachers in the South are, and we don't want it to backfire on us in the public eye," Paul warned. After that they began to look at the photos and decided they needed a forensic expert to do so as well and tell them if their assumptions were correct. Paul then left to go back to Cleveland to prepare the necessary affidavits to get a search warrant for the pastor's car, office and home from Judge Baoini, promising to let Taylor join in the search when the warrants were executed.

That afternoon, Paul presented the judge with an affidavit that laid out Weasel's story about where the rings were found and Paul's theory that other evidence may well be found in the study of the pastor, his car as well as his home, the church parsonage, just a short distance from the Church on Interstate Road. Though Judge Baioni had doubts as to the necessity of searching the vehicle, he issued warrants for all three requested places. Paul then called Taylor to line him up to search the vehicle first, then the study, then the home, all in the morning at 8:00 a.m. Both were excited as they had been in quite a while. At the prearranged time, Paul and two Bolivar County deputies, including Joel, met Taylor at the pastor's home where they found his car parked in the gravel driveway. The search of the interior of the vehicle revealed nothing, but the warrant allowed them to take their time and measure each tire's width, and closely photograph the tread of each tire for comparative purposes with the crime scene photos of the tracks. They then moved to the interior of the home. They were about to wrap up their search there when Joel came across an item of interest: A small faux diamond dog collar lying inside the closet of the master bedroom. It was tagged and bagged and taken by Taylor for use in the Garrett prosecution. Paul had a hard time getting excited because he had seen a small rat terrier dog on the screened in porch earlier and knew it would be argued that he had bought the collar for his own dog. That was of course, until he found the name, "Pips", engraved on the collar. The search moved on to the pastor's study. All present checked books, drawers in file cabinets and desks as well as waste baskets throughout the office. Joel hit pay dirt he believed, when he produced a small golden chain on the floor under the desk. The chain itself had been broken, and no charm was attached, but it too was tagged and bagged and retained by Taylor for Sunflower County's use. The searches completed, the Bolivar County boys all agreed that with Weasel's testimony, they had probable cause for an arrest and couldn't wait to interrogate the pastor. When Taylor explained to them the significance of the two items he had found, they all agreed that the preacher was toast in Sunflower County and probably in Bolivar as well. They would let their respective bosses and district attorneys talk about and hopefully agree who would try the bastard first. They all left with visions of arrest warrants on their mind. A young boy held the key to the Bolivar prosecution like before, but even if the pastor managed to cheat death in that case, Sunflower County was waiting with enough physical evidence that didn't hinge on any one person's testimony to bury him. They would pick him up on behalf of both Sunflower County and Bolivar County tomorrow, God willing.

Paul headed straight to his office to prepare an affidavit for the arrest of Reverend W. D. Kirksey for the murders of Linda Strawberry and Janice Galtelli. Taylor was busy doing likewise for the murder of Jennifer Garrett. Both had agreed to contact the other when warrants were issued to coordinate the arrests. Landon Fall talked with Frank Carlotta in Sunflower County, the district attorney in that district and they agreed that Bolivar would be spotlighted with Sunflower playing it lower key when the arrest was made to help with the general political climate concerning the length of time since the murders in Bolivar. But after indictments, Bolivar would try the man first and if he wasn't satisfactorily convicted, Sunflower would come in and clean up. Such was politics in the South and particularly the Delta. Sure enough, both counties' secured arrest warrants that night and both agencies converged on the Interstate Baptist Church at 8:00 a.m. the next morning to arrest the defendant on two counts of capital murder for which the death penalty would be sought. Law enforcement personnel was not the only ones present at the church that morning, however. Having seen the contingent of police vehicles at the church that morning, young Weasel Bowman had ridden his bike to the church to investigate. He waited on his bike next to Paul Lane's car that he easily recognized and was still there when W.D. Kirksey was led out of the church with his hands cuffed behind his back. As they neared Paul's car to place him in the backseat, Weasel moved his bike out of the way, smiled broadly and waved to the Pastor and said, "Hey, Preacher, Randy says your life may be in danger," and then slowly rode away from the church heading back home, all the time crying to himself, but never looking back.

CHAPTER 33

The pastor was transported to the Bolivar County jail at the courthouse in Cleveland and booked into the freshly vacated cell that belonged to Raymond Butler just a day or so earlier before his release. Though his life as he had known it was over without question, regardless of the verdict in the future, Paul looked at him and thought the preacher wore a smirk on his face as if trying to convey the message to the public that he was without fear of the situation. Either way, Paul knew he had to talk to Taylor Buttrell over in Sunflower County and let him know the pastor was in custody and held without bond for the present time. He already knew from deputies from Sunflower County who was present at the arrest of the defendant at the church earlier, but Paul wanted to let him know a first appearance and bond hearing would be set for the next day at nine a.m. in Cleveland. Taylor assured him if the bond was set too low, he would seek a higher bond on the Sunflower County murder charge even though it would mean holding him on Sunflower County's pay after transporting there from Bolivar. Hopefully, it would not get to that point.

Taylor knew his first order of business was to get Sammy and Wilma Garrett into his office and explain the latest developments. He set up a meeting with them the that day in his office right after lunch and asked Paul Lane to attend as well so he could assure them of the coming prosecution and procedure in Bolivar County as well. He agreed and everyone looked forward to the meeting in Indianola, Sunflower County, at one p.m. in Taylor's office. In the meantime, Paul contacted the Galtelli family at their home in Jackson and Estelle Strawberry at her home in Interstate. The Galtelli family members were unaware of the arrest of the pastor, but Mrs. Strawberry was well aware that the pastor from her own church had been arrested for the murder of her oldest daughter. So was everyone in Bolivar County and the news agencies would take the story state wide in a matter of hours. Some people took the news with a grain of salt after only recently having heard that Raymond Butler was arrested and then freed from the same charge only days before. Quietly, Paul wondered if the fact that they had been wrong about Raymond would hinder their efforts to obtain a conviction against Kirksey. Only time would tell. He could hear the press and the defense lawyers now saying or questioning his detective witnesses, "Are you as sure about W.D. Kirksey's guilt as you were Raymond Butler? What if you are wrong about this one? Are you trying to destroy another man's life just to get a conviction? Funny thing was, the defense could get a change of venue to another county for press coverage that might influence people's opinion against the defendant, but the state could not. That would be an issue they may have to deal with in the future, but certainly couldn't worry about it now.

At precisely one p.m. the following day, Paul Lane got out of his car at the Sunflower County courthouse in Indianola and proceeded inside to meet with Taylor Buttrell and the parents of Jennifer Garrett. A throng of people, one with a camera from WABG TV in Greenwood confronted him. A reporter yelled at him, "Mr. Lane, are you as certain of W.D. Kirkey's guilt in these murders as you were of Raymond Butler"? "What makes this different than Raymond Butler's prosecution", another asked? "If the Sunflower County case against him is stronger, why not try him here first with competent prosecutors"? Paul had no comment and waved the questions off. However, deep inside he knew that both he and Landon Fall's reputation as a prosecutor as well as their political lives hung in the balance. If W.D. Kirksey wasn't dead from execution over these murders, Landon and Paul's political life certainly would be. The trial could not come fast enough.

CHAPTER 34

Paul entered the conference room of Tylor Buttrell and was immediately introduced to the Garretts, both of whom showed signs of being emotional, particularly Wilma. "I have just explained to Mr. and Mrs. Garrett the events of the past few days and our procedural plan of trying Kirksey first in Bolivar County and then in Sunflower County, depending on the verdict over there. "Do you mean to tell me that there is a chance he might not even be tried for the murder of my daughter", asked Wilma? Taylor responded, "Well if he is convicted of two counts of capital murder over there and sentenced to death, it would be an exercise in futility to try to impose the death penalty over here. We can only put him to death one time." "So, the answer to my question is yes, there is that chance, she asked? "What if the prosecutors over in Bolivar County botch the case like they did with Raymond Butler", she further asked? Their reputation ain't the best, you know". "Then we will try him over here", responded Taylor. "I don't agree with that, she stated. I want him to die for murdering my child. Besides, what happens if he is convicted in Bolivar and the appellant court reverses it. He walks?", she asked.

"We would still have the option to try him here in Sunflower", stated Paul. "My daughter still plays second fiddle to the Bolivar girls.

Why are they more important?", she questioned. Both Taylor and Paul replied in unison, "They are not". Paul then asked to speak with Taylor outside the conference room and he agreed as the Garretts looked at them suspiciously.

"Considering our debacle with Butler and Mrs. Garrett's suspicious nature, I have no trouble in agreeing to let Sunflower go first", Paul suggested. "May not be a bad idea", Taylor agreed. "I guess we both have to clear it with our district attorneys, but I don't anticipate a problem. Do you", asked Paul Lane? "Absolutely", not replied Taylor. They went back into the conference room and informed the Garretts that they had agreed to try the Sunflower County case against W.D. Kirksey first at her request, subject to their bosses approval. "Good", she responded. If you will let the man out on bond, I can assure both of you that neither of you will have to worry about a trial for Reverend Kirksey", she added. Sammy quickly spoke up and said, "Wilma we have talked about that and we have always been law abiding people and always will be." "I know, Wilma added, looking directly at Taylor, but accidents do happen, don't they"? Paul and Taylor were both shocked at the obvious threat to a man's life from a lady like herself, particularly in the presence of law enforcement officials. They both bid the Garretts goodbye and escorted them to the front door of Taylor's office. When they had gone, Paul turned to Taylor and said, "I've seen bereaved family members who would gladly take matters into their own hands as she suggested if they thought for a second that the perpetrator would walk free. I really don't think she was serious, however." "Don't kid yourself, Paul, she was charged with aggravated assault against her first husband once for striking him with a baseball bat while he was passed out drunk after he came home and beat the hell out of her. Her husband declined to press charges after her father paid him some money for his medical bills and settled with him for her". "Her brother shot a nigger who was supposedly breaking into his car once. We didn't prosecute because it would have been useless. Nigger was on parole from Parchman for grand larceny."

"All I'm saying is, it's in her genes and on top of all that, she works for the post office," he added, almost laughing out loud. "Hate to prosecute her in this county if she acted on her threat, he said," with his voice trailing off. With that, they both headed home to talk to their respective DA's about their plan. They would both receive a green light from their boss.

CHAPTER 35

THE first appearance for W.D. Kirksey was set for the following Thursday at nine a.m. in Cleveland. Bolivar County would transport him from Cleveland to the jail and courthouse in Indianola if he possibly made bond on the Bolivar County charge and Sunflower County agreed to hold without bond after his transportation and until bond setting in Sunflower County. He had been appointed counsel in Bolivar but this would not guarantee the same attorney would represent him in Sunflower on the murder charge there, however, unless the Court there made that appointment at the appropriate time. He was immediately appointed an attorney at his first appearance in Cleveland. Clay Watson, a public Defender with the county was appointed by Judge Baioni to represent him through arraignment and beyond until further orders of the court. Watson was a seasoned criminal defense lawyer who had served as a public defender in Sunflower County for eighteen years. He had two things that people spoke negatively about in reference to him. One was the fact that despite being forty five years old, he still looked like an Ole Miss fraternity boy despite his best efforts to look more mature. The other was his penchant for a drink at the end of the day. This was really no big deal because most lawyers ended the day with a drink or beer at a local watering hole. Problem with Watson was, he sometimes ended his day at lunch or even earlier if the mood struck him. The fact that he looked younger than he was sometimes worked to his advantage as some lawyers underestimated his legal ability because of it and suffered the consequence accordingly.

When the case of ***State of Mississippi vs. W.D. Kirksey*** was called up by Judge Baioni, He stood at the Defendant's table with Watson, his hands shackled to his waist. With the advice of counsel, he entered a plea of not guilty to the charge of murder of Linda Strawberry and Janice Galtelli, but the entry of a formal pleas was unnecessary at this point, but would be requested later a formal arraignment. Paul surmised that Clay was playing to the press and the public by allowing him to do this to make it clear that his client was innocent. Clay Watson then asked that a reasonable bond be set until trial. District Attorney Landon Fall asked that the Defendant be held without bond. Watson argued that he was employed as a minister over in Bolivar County, had been a resident for many years there and was not a flight risk. He argued that a bond of $250,000 would be excessive under the circumstances. Landon Fall was just about to make the usual prosecutorial argument that a high bond was necessary to protect the public in general because of the heinous crime that the Defendant was charged and inform his honor that there were other serious charges expected very soon in another jurisdiction. As he began to elaborate on the expected charge, suddenly and without warning, Mrs. Wilma Garrett stepped into the middle aisle of the courthouse with Robert Gunthrie, her thirty-five year old son from her previous marriage by her side and said, "Your honor, as mother and brother of the victim in the case D A Fall refers to, we join in defense counsel's request for a low bond and further ask that the Court allow the defendant be released on his own recognizance." "That's right, your Honor. We make that request, added Robert. Judge Baioni was shocked and bewildered, not knowing exactly how to handle such a request. He asked that both members of the family sit down and he would consider their request. They immediately did so and the judge called both counsel to the bench. After asking both for comment, knowing their response, he announced to the public that he would set a bond of $200,000. Until such time as the defendant was indicted by the Grand Jury and would reconsider same upon motion by either party thereafter. Court was adjourned and the crowd in the courtroom dispersed with Kirksey being escorted to the booking room at the jail.

After being booked, fingerprinted and an additional mug shot taken, Kirksey was led to the jail and Watson was allowed to speak to his client. He wanted to know from his lawyer just how much it would take to get him out at this point. Watson wanted him to wait as long as he could before trying to bond out to see if he could get a reduction in the amount. He also wanted to know from the Landon Fall if he was aware the victim's family wanted no bond and what was going on. The church had sent word to the pastor that he was not welcomed back to the pulpit any time soon under the circumstance, which surprised absolutely no one. Watson left his client in his cell just as supper, consisting of hamburger patties, mashed potatoes and sliced bread was brought to him. He immediately headed to the Pool Hall Grill, a local bar there in Cleveland to end his day and then headed to Squirrely's Lounge, his favorite bar and grill for supper and some beer. In the meantime, he thought about the bizarre events earlier in the courtroom. He couldn't wrap his head around the family's request for no bond for the killer of their daughter and sister unless they meant him harm. Many people threaten it, but he never knew anyone that was really serious about vigilante justice in such a case.

Clay Watson called Landon Fall when he got to his office the next morning and asked about the Garrett incident the previous day in the courtroom. Landon denied any knowledge of her reasons for such a request, but promised to check with the detective in charge of the case over in Sunflower County, Taylor Buttrell to see if he could say. When told by Buttrell of Wilma's statements in his office with Paul Lane there, he could only speculate that she and her brother intended harm to his client. He added that he was unconcerned for Wilma's threats, but knew nothing of her son, but would have him checked out. "I don't see anything to be greatly concerned about", said Watson. "Nor do I", answered Landon. "Will you agree to her request," asked Watson? "Of course not," said Landon. "Gotta protect the public". "OK, answered Watson, but we will waive indictment, and I'll be filing a motion for bond reduction". "No problem", responded Landon, who immediately had Paul contact Taylor in Sunflower County and see how quickly they could get an arrest warrant to hold Kirksey there if he should bond out in Bolivar County.

Watson headed over to the jail to discuss his procedural strategy with his client. Waiving indictment was of little consequence, was not an admission of guilt and simply expedited some matters particularly in this case, a possible lower bond.

CHAPTER 36

Wilma Garrett and her son, Robert Gunthrie, sat at the breakfast table finishing up eggs, bacon and biscuits, all the while reliving the events of the previous day at the courthouse. "Even if they don't let him out without bond, at some point, he's going to be transferred for trial, some hearings or something, I just have to be ready when the time comes", he told his mother. Robert was a disappointment to his mother in many ways. He had been in trouble as a juvenile many times, either in school or out on the town where he had committed many misdemeanor offenses such as possession of alcohol, shoplifting, petty theft malicious mischief and even auto theft, the latter of which almost got him sent to training school as a juvenile. Later, he had gotten into numerous fights and destroyed public property such as road signs, barricades and other road equipment. He was a skilled mechanic and loved guns and shooting, but had never been in trouble for violent crimes other than assaults from fighting. Also, compared to her beautiful Jennifer who never got into trouble, Robert was the black sheep of Wilma's family. Sammy had little to do with him and Robert was likewise toward Sammy. He was just a problem kid an there was no two ways about it.

"I don't want you to get into major trouble in dealing with this man", Wilma told her son. "I want to see him punished for what he did to your sister, but not at your expense", she told him. "It's like this, Mama, if you want something bad to happen to him, it's gonna happen," he warned her. "Just don't take any unnecessary risks, son", she told him. She was very aware that with enough encouragement, Robert would do any dirty work she wanted done and thank her for asking. She loved his allegiance to her and manipulated him constantly because of it. They finished eating and the two parted ways for the time being with Robert heading off to his rented apartment in nearby Leland.

After Clay Watson briefed his client on his plan to have him waive indictment and hopefully get his bond lowered, and finding W.D. Kirksey was in full agreement, he scheduled a motion hearing for bond reduction after informing the Judge Baioni and Landon Fall they wanted to waive indictment. Once the former was accomplished, the Court set the motion for bond reduction for the following week. When contacted by Taylor Buttrell, Wilma and Sammy Garrett advised him they would no longer seek a bond reduction or oppose a higher bond, but would leave it up to the Court, further assuring him they didn't care if he rotted in jail in the meantime, a complete reversal from the earlier position they, or at least Wilma had taken in the Bolivar County proceeding. Circuit Judge Baioni was advised of this at the hearing, initially causing Watson some heartburn. However, he argued to the judge that the only position the victim's family had taken was earlier when they asked for the defendant's release on his own recognizance, therefore with no bond. They sat silently when asked by the judge in open court refusing comment. The judge, after hearing argument from both sides, then set bond for Kirksey at $100,000, severing in half his earlier bond. With the assistance of some staunch church members who supported him, Kirksey made bond the next day shortly after lunch. The Garretts in Roundaway as family of the victim were all notified. An arrest warrant from Sunflower County had yet to be issued.

Kirksey was lost without his church to go to, but he headed home and developed a routine of busying himself in the day and returning home around eight p.m. each night. Robert and Wilma never talked again about something happening to Kirksey,

Paul Lane called Taylor Buttrell early the next morning. "I have bad news, Taylor", he almost shouted over the phone. "W.D. Kirksey was found lying in his driveway this morning by a church member. He had been assaulted with a blunt object and had a noticeable skull fracture. The person who called our office says they did not disturb the scene, except to roll him over checking for signs of life. The sheriff's department here retrieved two empty Colt 45 malt liquor bottles, an empty package of Kool cigarettes and an afro hair pick at the scene. Pastor's wallet and watch appeared to be missing. He was transported to East Bolivar County Hospital here in Cleveland where he is in ICU in critical condition. He's alive for the moment, but doctors say he isn't close to being out of the woods", Paul said almost without taking a breath. It's hard to imagine how a little old lady like Wilma Garrett could physically do this, but just in case, do you have any idea where she was last night", Paul inquired? Actually, I do, said Taylor, "She and I both were at a prayer circle for her at Roundaway Baptist Church, put together by her Sunday School class. Both of us were there until ten or later". "From what you say was found at the scene, we should be looking for a black male, don't you think, Taylor questioned? "Either that or someone who wanted us to think a black male was involved," Paul interjected. "Check on Robert's whereabouts".

Later in the day, Taylor called Paul with the news. "Robert Guthrie has a clean alibi. Seems he was at Squirrrely's Lounge eating and drinking from eight o'clock until after midnight. Manager there knew him and vouched for him. Need to figure the

time of the incident. Unless very early when it was daylight, or very late, Robert is not our man," said Taylor. "Just got a call from the hospital", Paul interrupted. "They don't expect Kirksey to make it through the night tonight". "How many more will have to die before we close this case", Paul wondered aloud. It's like a bad record that just keeps playing.

ABOUT THE AUTHOR

Born and raised in Cleveland, Mississippi in the heart of the Mississippi Delta, the author is a graduate of Cleveland High School, holds a BSE. From Delta State University and a Juris Doctor from The University of Mississippi School of Law. He is in his thirty second year as a Chancery Court Judge for the 3rd Chancery District of Mississippi where he is now Sr. Chancellor. He previously served one term as County prosecutor for DeSoto County, Mississippi. He is married to the former Vanessa Hurt and together they have two children and three grandchildren. When not in Court or writing, he spends his time hunting.